SISTER · ANNA

Megan,

We are pleased by your graduation. May this be the beginning of a bright future. We wish a number of blessings in the future. We have done a number of things with you. Anne, Mom Butchen things with you. Anne, Mom is one of our favorite lovers. She enjoyed being with the young ones. May the story be an inspiration to you.

Peace,
Buddy & Janet Cliff

May 2000

SISTER ○ ANNA
God's Captive to Set Others Free

Dorothy Garst Murray

The Brethren Press
Elgin, Ill.

SISTER ANNA

Copyright © 1983 by The Brethren Press, Elgin, Illinois 60120
Printed in the United States of America

Cover design by Kathy Kline

Cover portrait of Anna Beahm Mow by Guy Wolek

Library of Congress Cataloging in Publication Data

Murray, Dorothy Garst.
   Sister Anna, one who wasted not God's love.

    1. Mow, Anna B.   2. Church of the Brethren—
Clergy—United States—Biography.   I. Title.
BX7843.M68M87   1983   286'.5   82-24335
ISBN 0-87178-796-2

To my grandchildren

        Mary Willard
        David
        Kristin
        Kimberly
        Sarah

Contents

Foreword by Eugenia Price   9

Preface   15

1 Window On the Eternal   19

2 The Insatiable Thirst   29

3 Pilgrim in Process   39

4 The Joy of the Spirit   55

5 Wisdom, the World and Holy Hilarity   68

6 Surrender   81

7 Mother . . . and More   96

8 Speaking the Truth in Love   106

9 "Talking on Paper"   126

10 Ambassador of God's Grace   140

11 The Wild Hope, the Faith Tremendous   157

Epilogue   171

Foreword

I have known and loved Anna Mow almost as long as I have known and loved Jesus Christ—thirty three years: half of my life.

Once you have treated yourself to this superb biography and have experienced Dorothy Garst Murray's comprehensive telling of Anna's world-wide spiritual impact, you will better understand why I have chosen here to write of her as Anna Mow, the very human being and Anna Mow, my friend. Of course, the joy and sustenance and hilarity and comfort of being her friend through all these years began with her sane, balanced spiritual impact upon my own Christian life. Jesus Christ, Himself, has without doubt made possible one of the rarest friendships I've ever known. Without our faith in Him, Anna and I might have found each other somewhat interesting as persons, but due to our diverse backgrounds, we probably would not have grown close.

As I recall, we loved each other from our first meeting, and from that meeting she has been my friend. She has helped shape my thinking, my faith, even my own estimate of my faith. I, like everyone else, hit emotional and physical and spiritual lows. More often than not, at these times, something Anna says snaps me back to reality and keeps me from indulging in wasteful self-analysis. She has managed, not only to accept me where I am and as I am, but to challenge me to do the same with myself. And never has she done this by flinging a text at me!

Anna is so imbued with the very spirit of the written Word of God that she can pass this spirit along *without quoting*—by merely being Anna. When I confide a fear to her, great passages of Scripture seem to unroll in my mind and heart when Anna, in that confident, reassuring voice merely says: "Well, you're human. Your fear is normal. But it doesn't lessen God, does it?" The direct question—"does it?"—causes *me* to think. "Of course," my heart agrees, "my fear doesn't lessen God." And in my being ring His words, not hers: "Fear not, for I am with thee . . . " Anna didn't "fling" the text at me. She allowed me to remember it myself, giving exercise and tone to my own spiritual muscles. She may be the only ordained preacher who has never once preached "at" another human being. I couldn't prove that, but I'd be the last to be surprised if it turned out to be true.

For half my life on earth, Anna has never once, even unintentionally, stood between God and me. Not even her shadow has fallen between us, because whether we discuss opera, politics, books or shared longing for time alone, the atmosphere is full of His light. There is no room for shadow. A reader once said to me: "Oh, I get goose pimples thinking how profound and holy must be the conversations between you and Anna Mow!" When Anna reads that here, she will hoot with laughter. We do have holy exchange, but to strive for it would be the last thing either of us would think about. We have no need to impress each other. We simply talk together and enjoy. *I can tell her anything.* Why? Because she honestly *doesn't* judge. It seems never to occur to her that it might not be true that the Father has, indeed, left all judgment in the hands of the Son.

Perhaps we have become so close humanly speaking because our public lives at times leave us both in dire need of the kind of comfort that comes from bare feet, no girdles and silence from the telephone and doorbell, and the ear of an *understanding* friend. She still speaks far more often than I, as I write more books than she. Both writing and speaking demand persuasion, effort on our part to convince, to make real, to lift up. But there are *no* demands in our personal relationship. Sometimes when we talk, I do most of the talking. Sometimes Anna. Always we are together—according to what comes naturally. We are simply free to be ourselves without excuses, without pretense.

I sit here at my desk some days—as does she at hers, because Anna isn't perfect either—burdened down with false guilt because we've appeared to neglect this person or that. We let our shoulders sag at the sight of those piles of unanswered mail. We often laugh together by long distance because the stacks of mail get so high sometimes that they literally get "typed off" the corner of our desks. This happens, of course, because we both still use noisy old manual typewriters that literally jolt the room. "Oh, gracious," I've heard her say after a lengthy speaking schedule, "I haven't even read them all yet!" We are simply able to be ourselves with each other devoid of the burdensome self-consciousness that wrecks friendships.

We don't spout spiritual platitudes, we just talk.

She doesn't attempt to sound like a "spiritual leader" with me and I know I have never once faked it with Anna. I don't have to. She began with me where I was. She goes on loving me exactly where I am.

We share insights. We share loss. For years, we have shared publishing rewards and disappointments. We share music and plays and books and opinions on presidents, prime ministers, governments, politics, our mutual and total opposition to all war; we share talk of history and the organized church *and* the Body of Christ. She taught me once and for all that the organized church and the Body of Christ are not necessarily one and the same.

Lately, she lost a beloved sister. This same year I lost my only brother and my mother. We have shared grief. I don't recall her ever having given me a lecture on how to look at death, but through the years, by example, she has taught me that it can be taken in stride. While grieving with me, she could say and get my immediate agreement: "We will *celebrate* your mother!" When now and then the subject of our own physical deaths comes into a conversation, she is so naturally casual about hers that even on long distance, I can hear her smile. She never bores anyone with a "would be spiritual" sounding eagerness for heaven. She's simply eager for everything God has up ahead for her. She will delight in heaven, but she is equally eager to go on showing Him "plain" here on earth.

Naturally, we share laughter. Anyone whose life has ever touched hers, knows of her delicious humor. Yet, for her, tears of understanding come as easily as that laugh. She has shown me again and again how thin is the line that separates sorrow from joy—God's kind of joy. God's kind of sorrow.

Invariably she ends a letter to me or a telephone conversation with "*Bless* you!" I love it that she always emphasizes the word "bless." And then, almost always, she adds—"*Bless* your writing!" In many ways, she knows me better than I know myself and surely she knows and accepts in me that unlike her, where writing is concerned, I am single-tracked. Unlike her, I don't do well with unexpected guests or calls or too many demands on my time that keep me from writing. Writing books—books that should be required reading for every person attempting to live adequately—is only one thing Anna does. Her scope is almost beyond belief. Prodding has only once been a part of our friendship. I confess I did prod her—I prodded and prodded—until she agreed to talk with a publisher about putting her God-given wisdom and love and perception into print. I knew that even Anna couldn't hop enough planes or climb into enough automobiles to reach the numbers that books reach. Readers heeded her *naturalness* before God. She dived right into writing books making no more fuss about it than to say somewhat wistfully after a glance at the calendar: "Gracious, I wonder if I'll make it."

She has never prodded me that I remember. Anna is the only close Christian friend who has never once even hinted that I need to be more "this" or more "that." She is a believer in *God*. She leaves me to Him. Not in the process granting me license, rather, showing me that she respects the fact that I am a believer too. That I'm far more apt to listen to Him than to any human being. Even Anna Mow.

I am far from being her only close friend. We are scattered to the corners of the earth and she has ample room for us all. Easy, comfortable, Anna-room. In this remarkable book, you will come to know some of her world-famous friends, but you will also learn of the unknown young man who said that he loved Anna Mow because she was the only person he knew who "had it all together." Dr. E. Stanley Jones, Madam Pandit, Nehru's sister, Nels Ferré, Malcolm Muggeridge—these are some of Anna's many good friends. The famous names do not impress her, however. To her, names are merely a means of denoting one person from another. God's people have scared me for years because they seem at times almost to worship celebrity. Anna Mow loves people because God loves them—even when she can't remember their names. She loves and forms friendships with the dignity and perceptiveness and delight of God Himself.

As with Him, she loves us *as we are.*

With all of me, I urge you to read and reread Dorothy Murray's *impossible* biography of God's friend, Anna B. Mow. Impossible? Yes. Skillfully, perceptively, and after infinitely careful research, Dorothy Garst Murray has, in my opinion, done the impossible. She has managed to capture almost all of Anna in mere words—*and* the relationship between Dorothy and Anna has been a joy to observe. Words grow stubborn for me when I attempt to express my admiration for what Dorothy has done here. Feelings run so strong where Anna Mow is concerned that as I have read this book, I have shared Dorothy's occasional sense of trepidation as she wrote. She will know what I mean because she also knows that Anna Beahm Mow cannot be wholly captured except by her Lord.

I can promise you, the reader, that you will never forget the "impossible" piece of writing that Dorothy Murray has managed, nor will you forget my friend, Anna, who most of all, cares that you never forget her Friend, Jesus Christ.

Eugenia Price

Preface

Every once in a while there flash across the vast heavens of humanity a limited number of human beings who shine a little brighter, twinkle more audaciously and leave the universe a warmer and lovelier place for their having been. Out of the celestial mists they come, into the celestial mists they go, but in their brief trek across the space they inhabit they tend to stand out as clearly and sharply as Venus on a cold winter night. Most such persons have some unique characteristics. They refuse to be squeezed into the earth's mold. They are drawn to people and people are drawn to them. They appear to have a secret for living which is a bit beyond ordinary human knowledge. They appear to be truly "at home" in the universe.

Such a person is Anna Beahm Mow. Mother of three, grandmother of nineteen and great-grandmother of six, she was a missionary in India for seventeen years, a seminary professor for eighteen years, and the author of ten books and numerous published articles. This remarkable woman is still lecturing at eighty-nine years of age and scheduled two years in advance for speaking engagements.

The chronological order of her life has been followed to some extent in this book, but the chapters of the book are primarily related to her major activities, beliefs and interests. Chapters 1 through 3 cover the early years of her life: her childhood, education and the years of service in India. An experience she had in India made a profound impact on the remaining years of her life. Chapter 4 is devoted to the Holy Spirit: the impact of the Spirit on Anna herself and her conviction concerning the role of the Spirit as a living and viable advocate for Christians in today's world.

Her work as a teacher and scholar and some of her basic beliefs and methodology are covered in chapters 5 and 6. Relationship was a key word in her life and chapter 7 deals with the importance of her relationships: with God, with family, and with all her fellow human beings. Chapters 8 and 9 are given to those activities which are most familiar to the general public: her speechmaking and writing. Although many persons have become familiar with Anna through her speeches and her books, there are few who are aware of the extent of her impact in these two fields.

Anna's life was not all given to work and serious contemplation. Travel was a time of rest and recuperation for her, and chapter 10 covers this aspect of her life. Crisscrossing the continental United States and Canada for speechmaking is a way of life with her, and having crossed the Atlantic more than 24 times before age 90 makes her a bona fide member of the "jet set." Chapter 11 is a summation of Anna's passionately held belief that the teachings of Jesus Christ will one day be recognized as the only means of saving humankind from self-destruction, individually as well as collectively.

The writers of biography turn to numerous sources in order to capture an accurate word picture of their subject. The ten books Anna wrote were reread along with dozens of speeches, research papers written for graduate degrees and other articles she had prepared for publication. Newspaper and magazine articles about her which had been written by numerous persons provided further information. There were lengthy interviews with Anna herself as well as with three of her sisters: Sara B. Miller, Mary B. Baber and Lois B. Eyles.

These interviews gave insight into the childhood and family life that helped to form Anna's values. Hundreds of personal letters to Anna from students, co-workers, friends and relatives gave evidence of her impact on their lives. A number of persons with whom she had traveled, worked, lived and taught shared taped interviews with me. To each of these individuals—too many to name—I am grateful. I am indebted, too, to book editor Fred W. Swartz for his expert skill in helping to prune verbosity so that the manuscript might appear in a more acceptable printed form. Sincere appreciation is also due Eugenia Price for writing the Foreword, and to my husband Max for making my own writing possible.

Thomas Carlyle has observed that "a well-written life is almost as rare as a well-lived one." I have no illusions that I have written about Anna's life as well as she lived it, but I have done what I could. When told that I had been asked to write about her she cautioned me with her usual candor: "Now don't you go and try to make a saint out of me!" Her life stands as an adequate testimony to who she is and what she has done. It has been my intention to adhere to basic facts. No words of this writer nor those of any other are needed to elevate her to sainthood or to debase her as a mere mortal with clay feet. She is what she is: one who spent a lifetime striving to become more fully God's own person. With a discernment stemming from long years of living and loving she knew what *really* mattered—and she told the world about it in no uncertain terms.

Trying to capture the true essence of Sister Anna's life between the covers of a book is a little like trying to bottle a bit of a rainbow. Or like trying to capture the first sweet, heady fragrance of lilacs on a warm, rainy April evening. It just can't be done. But one must try. Why?

Because her life has made a bright, clear-cut statement to a confused and mixed-up world of what things are really important and what things are not. Because, as one of her youthful admirers declared, "She's one of the few people I've known who had it all together!" And, finally, because she might well be described as one of God's animated signposts to the kingdom of Heaven—and who of us doesn't need those signposts?

Dorothy Garst Murray
Roanoke, Virginia
October, 1982

Chapter 1
Window on the Eternal

"One of my earliest recollections was having my mother tell me how much she wanted me. She had lost her first baby at the age of six weeks and she was so happy when I was born and loved me so very much. She told me this over and over," Anna Beahm Mow said in a reminiscent mood. The words were scarcely finished when a younger sister broke in: "And do you know what she always told me? She said she wanted you so much because you were the first child and she wanted me so much because she hadn't had a baby for six years; and that because the two of us were wanted so much we had the best dispositions of all her children!"

The merry laughter that followed was tempered by the statement of the youngest sister when she said: "And she didn't want *me* at all and wouldn't look at me for an hour and a half, and Sara called me a polecat and wouldn't look at me for three days!" The peals of laughter that followed this poignant admission were softened by the assurance from gentle quiet Sara that Lois was soon loved and accepted by all and "had a very special place in our hearts because she was the youngest." At this point Mary laughingly reminded Lois: "I was even ready to give up my place as the baby and let you have the chicken livers from then on." She explained that while she was watching a nurse bathe the new baby she was told that from that day on she would never have another chicken liver to eat because they would always be given to the newest member of the family.

The small group of women recalling the recollections of their childhood included Sister Anna and three of her sisters: Sara B. Miller, Mary B. Baber, and Lois B. Eyles. Although their parents and two other family members were not present that bright November day in 1980, they were remembered in the many stories, the happy as well as poignant episodes, that were recalled. Another sister, Esther B. Hoff, was not present because of the distance involved. Anna's only brother, William, had died several years before after a long and distinguished career as a missionary to Africa and a teacher at Bethany Theological Seminary. Both parents were deceased.

All persons become what they are partly because of the genes of past generations, the family environment, their daily living experiences and the mores of the society and culture to which they have been exposed. It was soon evident that Sister Anna's exposure was not typical of that day. Her father, the Rev. I.N.H. Beahm, of German ancestry, was an ordained minister in the Church of the Brethren. Born at Good's Mill, Rockingham County, Virginia, in 1859, he was an educator and evangelist with a unique and individualistic personality. Having a phenomenal memory for detail, an insatiable desire for knowledge and a passionate devotion to his calling as a servant of God, he made some important marks on the graph of time, marks that were not always fully understood nor appreciated until examined in retrospect.

Anna's mother, Mary Bucher Beahm, was born in 1867, the daughter of a successful Pennsylvania Dutch farmer of Lancaster County. Sara recalled that their mother was teaching school at the age of 15 after having attended Lebanon Valley College and passing a teacher's certification test. She then decided to further her education in a "foreign" country, so off she went to Bridgewater College, over two hundred miles south! There she was taught by Professor Beahm who soon fell in love with his beautiful young student. They were married in 1890. From all future evidence she had a strong personality and a complete dedication to her career as a mother and a helpmate to her husband.

From the college they moved to Daleville, Virginia, where I.N.H. Beahm helped establish a small private school to provide a high school education for the children of farmers and businessmen in the small rural community. Here their first son, Goodwin, was born. He died shortly after birth. Anna (christened as Annie at birth) was born on

July 31, 1893.

Two factors were unique to the times in which the Beahm children were born and reared. It was an era of the "free ministry." Ministers in the Church of the Brethren were never paid a salary, and evangelists received no specific stipend. They made their livelihood by farming or some other endeavor and all church expenses were cared for by "free-will offerings." This often meant that an evangelist went home from two weeks of preaching and visiting with the warm feeling of having led some persons to God, but with the cold realization that these warm feelings would not be adequate to feed, clothe, and shelter his family. Three poignant entries in Brother Beahm's diary of the year 1895 reflect this burden on his heart.

He had recently moved with his wife and eighteen-month-old Annie to Lowry, Virginia, and they were waiting for their furniture to arrive as well as the imminent birth of a new baby. His diary entry on January 9 read: "Father dines with us and I sit on Annie's high chair, eat from a tin pot lid and use a paring knife and a spoon for my knife and fork. It is cheap to be poor but unhandy. P.M. I start a small bed for Annie. Feel just a little 'blue' but must come out of this. We ought always to pray and not to faint."

After a long day on January 15 in which his wife was having intermittent labor pains, he wrote: " . . . deliverance seemed approaching. We talked of sending for midwife then thought of sending for Dr. Decided to call in a colored woman of experience. She lived 1½ miles away. Bro. G.W. was sent for her in *Post haste*. But before he reached the house the new babe was born at 7:05. Mary and I were alone . . . When G.W. returned Mary and babe resting well. I was the doctor. At 7:30 I can say all seemed a success. Engage Aunt Sue Hogans to cook and attend mother and babe for $1.00 per week. Mary and I are thankful indeed . . . The Lord is good to us!"

Several weeks after the birth of the new baby, Sara, he went to Pennsylvania to conduct an evangelistic meeting. While there, he gave one of the addresses at the Philadelphia's Christian Reformers' Convention. He returned to Royersford where he preached again that night. Reflecting on the long, full day he wrote in his diary: "In buying my ticket for the city and back this A.M. I spent all my money but 12 cents. Think of a man nearly 500 miles from home having only 12 cents and expected to speak courageously to a State Convention of Christian Reformers!"

There were many other entries that indicated a deep need for doing what he felt he had to do as a minister and a teacher, yet indicative of the fact that he had a real concern for the hardship that this brought to his wife and family. That year he built a small home and many entries were made relating to payments on their home. On August 30 he made this entry: "Reached home and find my dear ones well. So glad to see them. Gone just four weeks. Left home with not quite enough money for my expenses to Father's. Was among the poor one-half the time. I returned home with several nice little presents and $26.00 in my pocket. The Lord will care for us. May we trust him more fully and work for him more diligently!"

Persons in the field of education fared little better financially than those in the ministry. Public school teachers were poorly paid. All too many of the early Brethren shared the philosophy of the brother who felt it his duty to "raise his children in pious ignorance" because he firmly believed that "ignorance is the safeguard of virtue" (diary entry Feb. 8, 1895). This indifference to education proved, in some cases, to be an almost fanatical dedication to the preservation of ignorance. Those persons who saw the importance of building schools and educating their children beyond grade school were in a decided minority.

Brother Beahm found himself in a double bind. His keen intellect and inquiring mind drove him into the field of education. He taught and helped to establish schools at both a high school and college level. And it was out of his genuine interest in the spiritual welfare of every person, as well as his love for preaching, that led him into the field of evangelism. Neither of these occupations provided the financial security needed by a growing family. Between the years of 1889 and 1907 he helped to establish and was principal of Botetourt Normal (later Daleville Academy); he was founder and principal of Prince William Normal,

Brentsville, Va.; was president of Lordsburg College in California (now La Verne University); and he was one of the founders, business manager and president of Elizabethtown College in Pennsylvania.

As a result of their father's educational and evangelistic involvements, the Beahm children were born, educated and reared in many different parts of the country. The sisters recalled with much mirth that Brother William "had his beginning" in Winchester, Virginia, but was born in Tazewell County where their father was teaching at the time. They also remembered that being in debt was a problem that caused real hardship at times because Father Beahm not only borrowed money to help get schools started, he also borrowed money to establish Churches of the Brethren in several of the areas where he was teaching.

Anna can recall vividly the beginning of the church in Lynchburg, Virginia. Her father was teaching there. Shortly after school started he brought together all the Brethren families in the area and they were soon meeting in the homes for worship. When the group grew large, he borrowed money to buy a vacant store building in order for them to have adequate space in which to hold services. "I remember Mother signing that piece of paper," Anna said. "She was hesitant, but she never felt she could do anything against what he wanted to do for the church." A half-century later Sister Anna was asked to preach at the 50th anniversary of this church which now has a beautiful church building and a well-established congregation. She recalled how deeply moved she was to see that same piece of paper in such a different light fifty years after it had been signed by both her mother and her father.

This same scenario was repeated in several places in regard to the establishment of both schools and churches. Mary laughingly recalled that they sometimes accused their father of "tithing for the family and giving the balance to the Lord's work." All of the sisters agreed, however, that the heritage given them by their parents was one which could never have been bought at any price.

Theirs was the heritage of a hospitable home. It was a home with a world outlook and as such reached out to all of humanity. "Anyone was welcome at our home," said Anna, "and our mother could make the best meals that you can imagine out of the simplest foods." They remember especially her shoo-fly pies, homemade egg noodles and pretzels because few of their little Virginia friends were familiar with these Pennsylvania Dutch delicacies. "And we were being fed nutritionally long before most people even knew what the word meant," added Mary. They ate according to the advice of *The Ladies' Home Journal*: succulent vegetables, fresh fruit, prunes, oatmeal and whole-wheat bread. The foods being "discovered" today by the health food faddists are the foods they ate because they were cheap and plentiful.

The *Journal* was Mother Beahm's window on the world. She was one of the original subscribers. Even their father took an interest in the *Journal*. On an icy, wintry morning, March 16, 1895, he visited the *Journal* offices in Philadelphia and that evening noted in his diary: " . . . Went through from top to bottom. Quite a business. Saw Mary's name there . . . Edward Bok's room is a most beautiful one. Many pictures, flowers, books, a kind of blue Brussell's carpet, etc." The magazine not only provided creative ideas about how to be a better cook and raise children, it also opened up a whole wide world of other people and cultures. Anna remembered that reading secular articles about India stimulated her interest in going there as a missionary long before the church ever challenged her with this possibility.

Their mother's interest in the royal families of Europe was not just an idle curiosity about how such persons lived; she cared about them as persons. When Alexis, the only son of Tsar Nicholas II and Empress Alexandra of Russia, was born with the dread disease of hemophilia in 1903, Mother Beahm prayed for his recovery right along with the well-being of her own children. When Queen Victoria died in London the Beahms mourned with her royal subjects because they *cared*. This example taught the children there was a world beyond the perimeter of their daily lives and that a loving God cared for the well-being of all the human family. His love extended all the way from the royalty of

Europe right down to the drunk roomer who once sat on their front steps. Small Esther lovingly embraced him and declared emphatically: "You aren't 'gunk' are you, Mr. Hall?" This seed of compassionate concern was probably planted by their preacher father but it was surely watered and nurtured into maturity by their mother and what she learned from the *Journal* as well as from life.

In addition to the magazines, there were walls lined with books. Most were religious books and the classics. "We didn't have as many playthings and as many fine clothes as some of our friends but we always had more books, no matter where we lived. Our house was usually the only house in the village that had a room called the library, and sometimes our little friends would want to come in and just look at all the books that lined the walls," Lois recalled. It seemed to I.N.H. Beahm's children that their father knew what was in most of them, too. He had memorized the entire book of Isaiah and many other passages from the Bible. He also had committed to memory much of Shakespeare and selections from other literary classics.

Father Beahm taught every one of his six children at some time in their school careers. All of them fully agreed that his was the most interesting class they ever had. He made the material he was teaching come alive for his students. It wasn't always fun being in his classroom, however. They felt he often bent over backwards not to show favoritism to his own children. He expected hard work and diligent application from all of his students, especially from his children.

Reading was a favorite pastime for all members of the family. "We were never bored like so many children seem to be today," said Lois, "because there was a whole vast world to be discovered in our books. And we had to put forth some effort to participate in the discovery." The funny papers were taboo, though, because their father did not approve of the slang language used there. Mary and Lois gleefully recalled, however, that they had read stacks and stacks of "funnies" at a black neighbor's home. She had saved them for all the neighbor children who came to visit. Small Lois' ability to read was so sharpened by this exercise in reading the funnies that she astounded one of their neighbors by how well she read. When the neighbor commented on her reading ability Lois airily replied: "Oh, I can read *without* the book." And she demonstrated this unusual ability by reciting an entire story—from memory.

Theirs was a heritage that taught adaptability, responsibility and hard work. Moving frequently meant adjustment to new schools, new friends, new social mores. These children learned early to be at home anywhere because of the security found in their parents, in each other, and above all in God. Their mother had some physical problems which affected her health adversely, and all of the children learned early to carry their share of the load. Anna was only 16 when Lois was born, but from that day forward she assumed complete charge of meal preparation and cleanup. "I have a crooked hip today from carrying Lois around while washing dishes," she shared good-naturedly with her characteristic laugh.

Not all was hard work. There was a heritage of fun, too, and a love for *quality* in life even though there was not always *quantity*. Mother Beahm, mindful of the girls' need to look nice, made the loveliest dresses possible from the best quality of woolens and sheer, beautiful zephyr ginghams that were bought by the bolt at local mills. Sister Anna made her first dress at the age of 13, and from then on she made many of her own clothes as well as those of her sisters and her children. Some of the dresses were made over from hand-me-downs, but their mother's flair for making things beautiful usually made them turn out quite all right. Anna remembered one especially lovely gray wool dress she had which was trimmed in red velvet. It had been salvaged from one of her mother's own girlhood dresses. This dress caused some consternation in their local church because some of the women wondered "how in the world these children could afford to wear such expensive dresses when their father was just a preacher." The church women did not recognize the love, the resourcefulness, nor the innate wisdom that Mother Beahm had in instilling a healthy sense of pride in her girls for their personal appearance.

Doing the same for her husband was another story,

however. In his efforts to never appear better dressed than those to whom he was preaching, he was known on occasion to change his clothes, putting on an old, threadbare suit before going into the pulpit in some of the small country churches where he often preached. One of the favorite family jokes concerned Brother Beahm's determination to not "outdo others in dress." One of his sisters, thinking he really *should* have a nice suit in which to preach, went to a tailor and selected some handsome woolen material for the making of a dignified Dunker minister's suit. She paid for the material and paid the tailor for making the suit. Whereupon, I.N.H., not to be outdone by this conniving female, went down to the tailor and told him he needed the money a lot more than he did the suit. The tailor obligingly returned the money which, in the name of the Lord, of course, Brother Beahm gave to a small, struggling country church. Such dedication to egalitarianism and living by the rules of the simple life may be smiled about in today's throw-away economy but at the time it was sometimes a source of embarrassment for the family.

The recalling of this and other similar episodes was softened by the Beahm blessing—their hearty sense of humor. As Anna and her sisters reminisced about their childhood, the zestful laughter shared was indicative of this priceless possession. They spoke with joy of the many games they shared: word games such as Logomacky (a forenner of today's Scrabble), Authors, and others. Dominos, checkers, Bible games, puzzles—these and others sharpened their wits and taught them to be good losers as well as graceful winners.

Theirs was a heritage where people and their individual relationships to a living and loving God were central. It was a religious heritage that recognized the need for continuous growth, a continuing search for truth, and a genuine respect for those persons who might have different religious beliefs and customs. Mary remembered that as a small child she was "frightened to death of burning in hell." Anna recalled being baptized because she was afraid not to. She also spent some sleepless nights because she feared she might die in her sleep; yet, she couldn't pray about this fear because she wasn't wearing her prayer veil. All of them agreed that most of these religious "fears" came from their little friends and from hearing some fire and brimstone preaching from other ministers. Neither their mother nor their father had instilled such fears, and once they talked over these ideas with them a clearer perspective was gained.

Family worship was a daily part of living and Anna declared she was grown before she knew that "inthenurtureandadmonitionoftheLord" wasn't one word. She had heard her mother pray daily: " . . . and help us, O God, to raise our precious children in the nurture and admonition of the Lord." There may have been some doubts in Anna's future years as to "who she was" but there surely was no doubt as to "whose" she was. And as Lois laughingly pointed out, "We never did have to waste much time finding ourselves because we were never lost!"

The discussion of family prayer time and its lasting influence provided another good story. Four-year-old Esther had been called on to lead by praying a prayer she had been taught. She forgot some of the words and Anna, trying to be helpful, prompted her. Esther rose from her knees, walked across the room to where Anna was kneeling, gave her a swift kick and loudly announced, "I can do it myself." She then returned to her place in the family circle, got down on her knees and she *did*. "That lesson taught me a lot," said Anna, "about respecting a child's right to do her own thing."

There are two kinds of people. They are described by the Latin phrases *sub specia aeternitatis* and *sub specie temporis*, literally those who live by the eternal view and those who live by the temporary. The former see themselves as a part of the great continuum of humanity, struggling to fulfill the Creator's overall plan for human destiny. Their reason for living is to find and fulfill their own infinitesimal part in the total design. The latter see life as temporary, worshipping the small gods of self-gratification and feeling little responsibility for their relationship with other human beings or with God. The here and now is all that matters. There is much concrete evidence that the Beahm family life was based on the eternal view. It was the solid foundation on which Anna had her beginning.

Chapter 2
The Insatiable Thirst

I.N.H. Beahm wrote in his diary July 31, 1895: "Annie is two years old today. She is not large but she is precocious of mind. She's pert and learns fast." Little did he dream that his precocious small Annie would one day be the author of ten books and the reader of probably 10,000 more. Little did he dream that she would become a teacher of such impact that many of her students would feel she made the deepest imprint on their lives of any teacher they ever had. Little did he know that one day her scholarly endeavors would cause her name to be followed by seven academic degrees and that she would be included in the eleventh edition of *Who's Who Among American Women*, the 1975-76 edition of *Personalities of the South*, the 1979 edition of *The World's Who's Who of Women*, the *Dictionary of International Biography* and several other lists of those who have made notable contributions to the contemporary scene. And to imagine that some day she would be having tea in the home of Malcolm Muggeridge, one of the 20th century's most prolific writers and scholars, would have been a fantasy beyond his wildest comprehension. His diary entry was made on a warm summer night after a busy day "helping in Sanger and Company's warehouse" and going for some strawberry plants to put in his garden. His entry closed with these words: "I feel my shortcomings and errors heavily. I need so much of the Christlife."

No doubt his own and his wife's oft-expressed need for the "Christlife" was so imbedded in the mind of this small, alert two-year-old that she couldn't do anything else but become a student, a teacher, a scholar dedicated to that same Way. The influence of those early years helped to firmly establish the concept that it was God's life, not her own, with which she had been entrusted. The gift of a good mind must be developed for the furtherance of His purposes in the world, not solely for her own ego satisfaction. Her parents' personal, passionate devotion to Christ no doubt instilled in her the idea that every life, including her own, was of value in achieving God's long-range purposes in the world. It is very doubtful that such noble and idealistic concepts were spelled out in specific terms to one so young, nor that they were even talked about in her presence. However, as Sister Anna commented in her 88th year, "It was the very air we breathed." Born with a native intelligence second to few, nurtured in an atmosphere that produced an insatiable thirst for knowledge, it was only natural that she should become an apt student, a worthy teacher and a lifelong scholar.

Her early schooling took place in the public schools and the small private seminaries and academies that were established to provide high school studies for those living in rural areas. Her high school work was finished at Hebron Seminary, Nokesville, Virginia, in the year 1914. There were five students in the graduating class of this small seminary that had been established by her father.

Those early years of education were not easy ones. Because of her mother's failing health much of the responsibility of family care fell on the shoulders of the older sisters. Study had to be sandwiched between the household chores and the care of younger children. Not only was young Anna involved in the care of her sisters and brother, she also helped take care of young cousins. In the summer of 1904, the year she was eleven years old, she was sent to Caroline County, Maryland, to help her Aunt Annie King with her new baby, Esther, who had been born the previous February.

The Kings lived on a large farm. With the new baby, meals to prepare for the family and hired help and many, many farm chores, the work load was heavy and must have seemed endless to the young mother and her little helper. But apparently young Anna was equal to the challenge for she was asked to come back for the following two summers to help care for Samuel, born in 1905, and Bernard, born in 1906. According to Esther (now Mrs. Clifton Crouse), "My mother often told us Cousin Anna was a great help . . . She seemed like part of our family, and as I grew older, each summer brought some of our Beahm cousins to the farm. Even William spent several summers with us. I remember the summer when I was eleven my mother took me and my baby sister Anne on a long train trip to visit Aunt Mary and her family at Nokesville, Virginia. It was only 100 miles away — but it took all day! Between our farm and Nokesville we had to change trains in both Baltimore and Washington."

Those years of helping to care for her own brother and sisters and the King children probably started Anna's deep-seated love for children. The example of a loving mother and her beloved Aunt Annie King left little doubt in her mind about the importance of stable family life. In her late teen years, however, she began to feel the urge for independence, for making a life of her own. At the age of eighteen she felt a definite leading in the direction of becoming a missionary, preferably among the children of India. The obstacles, however, seemed insurmountable. There was no money for further education. Her father was away from home much of the time in evangelistic meetings, and her mother's health was poor. The burden of carrying out the family responsibilities rested primarily upon the shoulders of the older children.

One can imagine the frustrations that must have been felt at times by one so filled with the ambition to study and to serve yet with so little hope of realizing her dreams. But "where there's a will there's a way" was more than a mere copybook maxim for this strong-minded young woman. She had the will; she had absolute faith that if God wanted her to go to India as a missionary a way would open up. It did, step by step.

In the fall of 1914 she entered Bethany Bible School in Chicago, from which evolved Bethany Theological Seminary, the graduate school in theological training for the Church of the Brethren. Just before leaving for school she went to her mother's bedside to say good-bye. "I left my mother with mixed feelings," recalled Anna. "She was bedfast most of the time by then and the war had just started in Europe. I remember asking her which side we were on!"

Then she added, "I had my train ticket and forty dollars in my pocket. In later years I could tell my grandchildren and other youth that when I arrived in Chicago I had forty dollars. After seven years I had two degrees, a husband and fifty dollars. That's part of my faith story!"

While at Bethany she was given enough work to pay her school expenses. At the end of her first year; President E. G. Hoff called her to his office. He told her that he and two other faculty members had a weekly prayer service in which they prayed for guidance concerning the school and each of the students. Each of the three, individually, had been led by divine guidance to believe that she should cancel her plans for the mission field and prepare herself as a teacher so that she could help in their school. "I was stumped," she recalled. "All I could say was that I would consider it. I surely didn't want to be in India if God wanted me in America."

She knew that a college education was necessary whatever she chose to do, so the next step was to look into that. But after examining several college catalogs and determining what the approximate cost would be, she decided that a college education was simply out of the question. There was no possible way that it could be financed, to say nothing of the fact that she felt she was needed by her family.

Anna had a custom of walking often in nearby Garfield Park. One Tuesday morning after finishing her morning meditations she walked to the park. As she walked, she pondered how she might best know God's plan for her life. Suddenly a question came to her with startling clarity: "How dare you decide against college without asking God about it?" "And so," recalled Anna, "I apologized to the Lord and said: 'If You want me to go to college You will have to open the way for me!'" On Friday of that same week she received a letter from Dr. Otho Winger, president of Manchester College in Indiana, offering her a position that would cancel every expense at Manchester until she graduated!

She entered Manchester that fall. Although she had a job that would take care of the actual college charges, there was no money for incidental expenses. "But," chuckled Anna, "God took care of that, too. Every time I was penniless I remembered a greeting card I had received the first Christmas I was in Bible school in Chicago. I had run out of money just before Christmas with no time to earn more until after the holidays. This was awkward, to say the least. Imagine my surprise when just before Christmas I received this card from an old man in Virginia. All he knew about me was that I wanted to be a missionary. He had been a guest in our home the day before I left for Chicago. On the inside of the card he had written: 'The Lord put it into my mind and heart to send you this. Thank Him for it!' And he enclosed a money order for five dollars! The words were worth even more to me than the money. It was comforting to think that God kept track of my pocketbook, too." And He did keep track, good track. Another time Aobow, a Chinese student who was in the Sunday school class Anna taught at the Bible school, slipped an envelope beneath her door containing a five-dollar bill and a note saying simply "From God."

These expressions of love now found their way from Chicago to Manchester as gifts came from many sources to help with her college expenses. "Once," said Anna, "I actually couldn't write home for six weeks because I didn't have money to buy postage." But always when things were too difficult financially another "gift from God" would arrive via one of His faithful servants. For example, Moy Gwong, another Chinese friend from the Bible school days, was preaching occasionally at Anna's home church; but he refused to accept any money for his services, asking that it be sent instead to Manchester College where it could be applied to Anna's incidental expenses. Apparently the same thought had been put into the hearts and minds of many persons, for when she graduated from Manchester in the spring of 1918, all bills were paid and there was enough money left over to pay for her diploma. God did, indeed, keep track of that pocketbook!

She returned to Bethany in the fall of 1918 to pursue further graduate studies in preparation for India's mission field. By this time she felt firmly convinced that this was where God was leading her for service. But there was to be further testing, testing that evoked deep emotions, required rational thinking, and demanded some fervent praying. Her closest friend at Bethany was Anetta C. Mow. Anetta had a brother, Baxter, who was a Rhodes Scholar at Jesus College, Oxford University, in England. After three years of study at Oxford, he had come to the Bethany campus to take further graduate work while teaching a class in Hebrew.

Baxter was interested also in the possibility of going to a foreign field in mission service. This common interest, their mutual love for Anetta, and in all probability the hand of the Almighty himself led Anna and Baxter into a courtship that eventually resulted in their engagement and the announcement of plans for marriage. When this became known to the faculty members, the three who had discouraged her interest in the mission field felt that she might be "foolishly choosing marriage instead of God's will." In Sister Anna's scheme of things, love for a mate, having a home of her own, and having children could and should come within the context of God's plans for her life — and that was that. But this had to be tested, too.

Shortly before their wedding date both of Baxter's parents became ill. Baxter told Anna that as the only son he felt an obligation to stay in America to care for them since there was no one else to whom they could turn for help. "Here it was again," said Anna. "I still felt I should go to India. The conviction by this time was unshakable. Baxter wrote to his parents saying he would stay in America to care for them, but he did not tell them it would cost him his marriage. For a week we faced the possibility of losing each other. Then a letter came from his father which said 'We will die in the poorhouse before we let any child of ours stay home from the mission field to care for us.' So then I *really* knew I was willing to put God ahead of my own desires. You see, if we put Him first He keeps something steady on the inside of us which holds us against all kinds of storms and pressures without."

There is an interesting postscript to the feelings of guidance the three faculty members had about Anna. After becoming a wife, a mother, and giving seventeen years of service as a missionary in India, she returned to the Bethany campus to teach eighteen more years. She was right and so were they. It was just one of God's interesting "sidetracks" that was a part of the overall design.

Plans for their wedding were of interest to many others besides the three blessed seminary professors. There were the four younger sisters and brother, all intensely interested in the wedding plans and having a new member of their family. There were dozens of cousins equally as interested. One of their favorite cousins, Caleb Bucher, received a letter from his Aunt Mary (Anna's mother) telling about the forthcoming nuptials. She was now completely bedridden and had no hopes of seeing the wedding herself, but her delightful sense of humor had not been destroyed by the long years of illness. Dated March 14, 1921, the letter to Caleb contained much family news and many informative remarks about the new family member. Among them were several choice, descriptive phrases that Anna's family enjoyed repeating for years to come. She wrote:

> I have something interesting to tell you this time, and I'm willing for you to have a little fun out of it. You can tell all of the kinfolks around that you know something, and make them right curious awhile before you tell them. It is this—come close so I can whisper in your ear. On March 30, at 8:00 P.M. there will be a wedding in the chapel at Bethany ... Do you want to know something about your new cousin? He's big, not pretty to hurt, good and fine and he's smart. Not a bit proud ... Baxter was born in Indiana, lived in Idaho after he was 11. He graduated from High School and Idaho University. At the latter place he won the Cecil Rhodes Scholarship (ask your teacher what that is) and spent three years at Oxford University ... In June he and Anna will graduate at Bethany where he teaches a class in Hebrew. He is a preacher. He can keep still in 6 or 8 languages. You may tell your mother first and she'll help you plan about the fun. Your papa likes to tease, now let him have a dose.

Cousin Caleb wasn't the only one who had a chuckle over Baxter's ability to "keep still in 6 or 8 languages." It became one of those cherished family jokes handed down for several generations. And if Anna's mother didn't think he was "pretty to hurt" he made up for it in later years, because in his nineties he is a distinguished and handsome gentleman who rides his bicycle about their home city with the ease of a teenager.

Their wedding took place in the Bethany chapel with President E. B. Hoff officiating. Following the ceremony they were presented with a beautiful guest book in which the minister had inscribed the following message:

> *Marriage is a sacred bond.* It is sacred because it is a vital part of God's creational program. It is sacred because by it two lives and hearts are united into one for greater joy and stronger service. It is sacred because it is thus that we establish the home—the fundamental and basic unit of society. It is sacred because by it we mutually duplicate ourselves for the future ages of larger opportunities and graver responsibilities. Will you *love, cherish* and *protect* each other and live together as *husband* and *wife* until death separates you?

And beneath the signatures of the two he had written and underlined:

> You are *husband* and *wife.*

Like all very solemn occasions there was a bit of humor, too. In a Beahm marriage there would have to be. Mary recalled more than sixty years later how much Anna's hand shook. "Why, I was sure she was going to drop her bouquet," laughed Mary, "and she was so white and pale I thought she was going to faint." In a letter written to Sister Anna many years later the organist for her wedding wrote:

> I remember the sound of your bridal shoes tramping that talkative wood floor of Bethany's old basement chapel! Clop, squeak, you were proceeding to your bridal vows. The rigor of those days ruled out aesthetics. There were no tall, white tapers, no mystical light from stained glass windows, no banks of ferns, no glory of a Bach aria ... Just the sound of your feet and the wonder of your smile ... To a person intimate to your congenial, consuming passion for the

Beautiful in Art, this picture of you in total radiance—
no matter what—spells out the most apt second
theme of your life . . .

With their June graduation from Bethany there was once again the rising hope that their joint dream of an assignment to the India mission field would be realized. But it was not to be—yet. Instead, they were sent to the Blue Ridge Mountains of Virginia to carry out a "home mission" assignment for the First District of Virginia. Soon Anna and Baxter were located in Rappahannock County in a little mountain village named Smedley. Having no car and being twenty-seven miles from the nearest railroad meant that there was plenty of walking to be done.

They set up housekeeping in a five-room log house for which they paid $1 per month for rent. Lest that seem a huge bargain, one must note that their salary was $23 per month—when it was paid. Some months the District could not even pay that amount, Sister Anna recalls.

Some of the professors at the seminary wondered how Baxter could possibly fit into such a rural setting with his brilliant mind and his many years of university study in large cities. They needn't have worried. When the men in this small community found that he could walk faster than any of them, could almost run up a mountain without becoming breathless, and most wonderful of all—that he could take "shortcuts" through the mountain hollows without getting lost, they were completely won over. "They really listened to him then," declared Anna, "they thought he was a god!"

And when Baxter picked, seeded and canned 30 quarts of cherries while Anna was on a trip to visit her family, the women of the community thought he was rather wonderful, too. He also picked enough wild grapes for his bride to make 30 quarts of grape juice. These "wild pickins" supplemented the many food gifts from the warmhearted mountain people, and the young couple had no problem with being well fed. It was there, where pumpkins were plentiful, that Sister Anna learned there are more ways to fix pumpkin than in pies. "About 595 different ways!" so she said. And when John Gidd's lovely gentle wife taught

Anna how to make what the Mows both declared to be the best sour-cream and soda biscuits in the world, their friendship with the people of the little mountain community was cemented permanently.

Their church house was a community-owned one and was used by both the Baptist and the Brethren ministers. According to the Mows' recollection: "On the Sundays that some of the Baptist ministers preached they gave a good 'dressing down' to the Brethren; and when some of the more conservative Brethren ministers preached they gave it right back." In fact, shortly before their arrival in Smedley, a fundamentalist Brethren minister had created quite a stir when he assured those in attendance that if they weren't baptized by trine immersion and if the women didn't wear bonnets and prayer veils, they would surely end up in hell.

Although there were some different theological interpretations, there was one thing on which there was unanimous sentiment. The hole in the side wall of the church was a mighty handy place through which they could spit their tobacco juice on Sunday mornings. And the members of one denomination seemed to be about as adept as the other in hitting that hole squarely from a good distance.

Their years of living at Smedley served as excellent preparation for their forthcoming years on the India mission field, because the warmhearted, frank mountain people were very similar to those they later would learn to know in the remote Indian villages to which they were sent. And it must have warmed the hearts of these people greatly when this young couple moved in and lived in their midst with such total acceptance of them, and with the assurance that there was indeed a more acceptable key to the kingdom of Heaven than they had been led to believe by some of the ministers who had brought them a more rigid interpretation of the gospel.

In September of 1923, Anna and Baxter received a notice from the General Mission Board of the Church of the Brethren that there was an opening for them to go to India. They had to be ready to sail in a matter of weeks. Their dream was to be realized.

Chapter 3
Pilgrim in Process

> Defeat may serve as well as victory
> To shake the soul and let the glory out.
> When the great oak is straining in the wind
> The boughs drink in new beauty and the trunk
> Sends down a deeper root on the windward side.
> Only the soul that knows the mighty grief
> Can know the mighty rapture. Sorrow comes
> To stretch out spaces in the heart for joy.
> —Edward Markham

The Mows' arrival in Bombay, October 1923, coincided with the Hindu New Year. A part of the festive celebration included hundreds of school children marching through the streets at night carrying lighted candles. The candlelit faces of the beautiful little brown children were a welcome that Anna and Baxter never forgot. There was symbolism, too, in their lighted candles. The young couple had come to bring Jesus Christ, the light of the world, to India. Yet they too would be given much about the art of living from their Indian friends. The light shed on their own lives in this alien culture taught them that the love of God was a two-way process: there had to be both giving *and* receiving.

The idealistic young couple soon found that this giving and receiving was not to be so simple as they had first perceived. Their arrival in India and their years of service there were concurrent with the chaotic upheaval which the nation was experiencing in attempting to achieve its political freedom. Missionaries serving in India at that time represented many faiths as well as many nations. They were expected to uphold the laws imposed by the British Empire which still ruled India. It was a time of painful transition for

India, and those who were there serving their various faiths were not exempt from the pain.

Gandhi, the leader in the nonviolent, noncooperative struggle for India's freedom from British rule, was beginning to be recognized throughout the world as a leader of great power with a totally new ideology about how to achieve political freedom without armed conflict. His philosophy of nonviolence and his wish to do away with the caste system had an especial appeal for the Mows who had been reared in a tradition which believed strongly in nonviolence as well as the dignity of all human beings. Anna felt that they were there to serve the cause of Christ and not the British Empire, and she had no hesitancy in expressing this sentiment as well as living by it. This soon brought her into direct conflict with some of the more experienced foreigners living there. Many of them felt just as strongly that it was necessary to adhere to the rules of those who were in political power even though the regulations might at some times rankle.

The Mows' close identification with the Indian people was a source of irritation to the "powers that be" in both the political and in some cases the religious institutions. It was during their years in India that both Anna and Baxter began to be aware of the need for the church to become the "body of Christ" in the world rather than becoming ossified within its own institutional framework. Their desire to serve those who were in no position to help themselves was stronger than their need to be accepted by those who felt it necessary to abide by the regulations of the hierarchy. The contrast between these two ideologies is revealed clearly in a letter written to Anna by one of the Indian Christians more than forty years after she and Baxter left India. He wrote concerning his first meeting with Anna and Baxter, which followed shortly after another missionary couple had visited in his home when he was a small child.

> . . . One such visit was paid by an Evangelist couple from North Gujarat. Their expected visit was announced in the church and so for days we children waited eagerly for their arrival, planning how we

would welcome them, talk to them and sing for them ... One fine morning they arrived, got off the cart, shook hands with the grownups and went straight into my father's office before we could even get a glimpse of them. That was frustrating for us children ... We vied with each other to get a chance to carry glasses of water to them ... I was fortunate enough to take some water to them. They did drink the water but they did not even look at me, leave aside the question of asking me who I was ... During the week they held many meetings, gave interesting sermons, took pains to teach us new songs and showed us "Magic Lantern" ... In the meetings they were very friendly and impressive but when they came home for food or rest it was next to impossible to come closer to them ... They came to the table when mother announced the food was ready, said grace in high-flown words which were not understood by us. They ate first with my father while my mother served. The lady Evangelist kept herself aloof and never once visited mother's kitchen or even appreciated the food she ate ...

... About two months after this, it was announced that Rev. and Mrs. Mow were to visit us. Once again, we children were excited and waited eagerly for your visit. The day came and we started arguing with each other as to who would go first to offer a glass of water. The bullock cart arrived and you two got off the cart and shook hands with my mother and father, while we, the children, were staring at you gawkeyed. Then suddenly the unexpected happened. Instead of walking away to my father's office, you two came toward us and started shaking hands with us and asking each of us our names. Then while Rev. Mow talked to my father, you, Mrs. Mow, gathered us all up and went to the kitchen where my mother had started preparing food. There you washed your hands, drank some water and sat down with my mother to help her in her cooking. While thus helping her you engaged the children by asking questions and collecting personal information on each of us. You even offered to bring your children with you the next time you came so that we could play with them. Halfway through the cooking my mother thought of sending us out and told us to go and talk with Rev. Mow. Still a bit apprehensive, we wondered how we could talk to such a big man. However, we followed mother's instructions and went out to find Rev. Mow walking about in the garden with an open knife in his hand, going from one plant to another, pruning a rose plant, cutting a dead leaf from a banana plant or cutting off some withered flowers from a Jasmine plant. When he saw us he turned his attention toward us, closed his pocket knife and amused us children with his tricks and pranks. That was something beyond our imagination. Anyway, we immediately took a liking for you two.

At mealtime we all sat together to eat and the prayers said by you were simple and not difficult to understand. We thought surely those simple prayers must not have taken long to reach the Almighty . . .

Small as I was, these two episodes kept bothering me for quite some time. I wondered: both of these pairs of Christian leaders were servants of God, both knew their Bible well, both were sincere about their jobs, both were learned and well-read! And yet . . .? Well, I could solve the puzzle later when I grew up and could think coherently. The first couple loved their job and worked sincerely for Christ, whereas the second couple loved their Lord and worked sincerely through Christ in their hearts. They actually lived for Jesus Christ.

Although this open and warm identification and friendship with the Indians was questioned by some of the foreigners, the Mows continued to minister freely to all who needed their help, including the untouchables. Through their children, who were friends and classmates at Woodstock (a boarding school operated by the British government), Anna became a close personal friend to Vijaya Lakshmi Pandit, a sister of Prime Minister Nehru. Both Nehru and Madame Pandit were politically involved in the freedom movement with Gandhi and both were jailed several times during this period. In the eyes of some, it was unthinkable that a Christian missionary should maintain friendship with a "jailbird." But for Anna, who had come to admire the staunch courage of many of Gandhi's followers, friendship and love were of far more importance than expediency.

There was one aspect of those early years of mission service that brought sheer joy, but it was joy mixed with heavy responsibility. It was the births of their three children: Lois Anetta, born April 24, 1924, at the Dahanu Road Mission Hospital; Joseph Baxter, July 10, 1926, in a military hospital at Landour; and David Merrill, December 25, 1928, at the mission hospital. Anna experienced the depths of Baxter's love just prior to Joe's birth. The attending Indian midwife insisted that "all my mothers have to take castor oil before delivery." Anna was equally determined that she would not take the castor oil because, according to her, it wasn't needed. Besides, she hated the taste. Baxter was with her and the two of them searched the room to see if there was some way they could dispose of the poured dosage. Finding no convenient way available, Baxter, noble soul that he was, swallowed the whole bit! "If I ever had any doubt about his love before," beamed Anna, "I didn't after that sacrificial experience."

But Anna and Baxter's love for each other, their love for their work, their love for God and for humanity itself was destined to face a period of trial by fire. Problems arose within the mission field family which posed the possibility that they might be sent home and not allowed to continue with their mission work. Misunderstandings flourished and grew, not only among the mission personnel but among the natives as well. Part of it centered around the usual human weakness of differing opinions about the mission program. Part of it stemmed from the political unrest which affected the natives and in turn affected the actions of all foreigners who were in India at the time. Most of it, no doubt, stemmed from the fact that they were just ordinary, weak mortal human beings working under extremely difficult circumstances.

The heavy load of responsibility relating to the mission work, the daily care of three active, imaginative small children in an alien culture, and the strain and stress of human relationships that were less than perfect began to take their toll mentally, physically and spiritually. Anna found her temper flaring and her patience tried beyond the breaking point on too many occasions. "I determined to conquer it," she said, "often spending much time in Bible study and prayer. But I would then come out from such an hour and say some cutting thing to someone, mostly in my home. I could control myself before others and that taunted me a lot. Baxter had reason to resent the 'spirituality' I was growing into. It had less and less of humility. It was getting to be a shell. I was irritated at my helplessness. I made myself more faithful in Bible study and prayer, but it was like beating the air. I blamed Baxter and others for my barrenness instead of blaming myself as I should have."

Anna continued to search for greater self-understanding and dedication during the two years the Mows were home on their first furlough. While Baxter taught a class at the University of Chicago, Anna worked in summer youth camps and visited many local churches in the interest of the mission program. She read insatiably after many of the contemporary religious writers and practical psychologists and attended numerous lectures and sermons in an effort to find some of the answers to her needs. She confided to a friend later: "I wanted God but I forgot the way, then one day I happened on the verse 'I am the Way, the Truth and the Life; no one cometh to the Father but by Me.' As old as that verse is, it struck me as if I had never heard it before." This, then, was the answer but the question still remained: how could Christ become more real to her?

After their return to India two small, unrelated episodes brought her face to face with the need for change in her own personal life. One day when she was irritable she scolded small Lois for something not very important that was not done properly. "I hurt her heart," confessed Anna, "and she looked at me with tears in her eyes and said: 'Mother, why can't you always be kind to me like Mrs. M— is to her little girl?'" It was a rebuke that caused Anna greater pain than any she had ever had. Another day she let herself fly at Baxter and he quietly asked her how the congregations she spoke to would feel about her messages of love if they could see her in such a mood.

Only a few days after these two episodes she was in a

Sunday school class at Landour taught by a Presbyterian missionary from Canada, Russell Graham. Graham asserted that if Christ were a living Presence in one's heart, one's family members would be the first to realize it because they know us best, know us as we *really* are. His message that morning fell on fertile soil in Anna's aching heart. "I knew then how very little I was before God, how measley I really was," she said later. She made a date to talk with Graham shortly afterward, and for the first time she was able to dump out all the many frustrations, questions and heartaches she had been experiencing in her quest for deeper spiritual growth and understanding. Their talk helped her to see there were sins that needed to be eradicated—among them her pride in her own self-sufficiency and her impatience with others who might not see things exactly as she saw them.

The talk with Graham helped and things went in a fairly satisfactory way for some months, but Anna still felt that she lacked the Something she needed to make her whole. Her search continued until the fall of 1934 when she was sent to New Delhi for a W.C.T.U. convention. On the way home she stopped at the home of the Grahams for a week of rest. In their home at Jaora they had a prayer room in a secluded part of the house and in the evenings the family and their guests gathered there for evening prayers and worship. It was during this week that Anna was to have an experience that would serve to alter her personality and change her life in such a way that not only her family would see the difference; the whole world would see it as years passed by.

She described this experience in a letter written to E. Stanley Jones. The letter was written at his request. They had been together in a spiritual retreat and Jones recognized that Sister Anna had had an unusual religious experience and he asked that it be shared with him in writing. The first part of this very personal letter described in some detail her early years and experiences as a young Christian, her and Baxter's years of work in India, and some of the problems with which she had been coping in terms of her own religious seeking and searching. This aspect of Sister

Anna's faith journey is so personal, so pertinent to her life's mission that it should be told by Sister Anna herself.

> In those evenings in the prayer room Mr. Graham led out, but all was spontaneous . . . Jesus seemed so real that it seemed I must open my eyes and see Him there with these eyes. The first evening the subject turned to the Cross. As we read the Word and meditated on it, it never was so real to me before. As I faced myself I realized more fully the barrier that still stood between me and my Lord . . . How I TRIED to take his unfathomable love but somehow I just couldn't. Kneeling at the Cross and being left out is awful, or rather *being* out. I had failed so many times I was afraid to take the step of faith which was involved in truly taking Him. I knew I had to have something which would make a REAL difference in my life and would manifest itself first in my home. But I was afraid to accept the possibility of that for such a stumbler as I had been. I was BOUND. I felt that if the next night we did not go to the Resurrection I would be crushed under the burden of the Cross. In the morning Mr. Graham tried to help me. He prayed, then he began to talk. And I found myself putting up a defense in my heart. I then realized that the very act of defense proved there was an idol still in my heart. I was willing to give it up—if necessary—but I was hoping it was not necessary. But I knew that anything I defended was in the way and that went, too. This made room for more peace, but how thankful I am that I did not feel full peace until I had the Great Gift.
>
> The next night Mr. Graham read *The Recall of Love* by Ralph Conner. Peter's stumbling, his experience during the dark days of the Cross and what the Resurrection meant to him were very vivid to me that night. After that he read John 20:1-23, hesitated there and read no further . . . After a session of prayer I felt the urge to reread that chapter. It seemed I could not get enough of it—the wonder of it all . . . When we were in prayer again, while Mr. Graham prayed I just felt that if he would lay his hands on my head and anoint me I would find freedom from the thing that bound me. It seemed I just couldn't let go . . . I did not

think of the laying on of hands without oil and I thought there would be no oil in that room and if I asked for it someone would have to go downstairs to get it and I did not want to trouble folks and so I decided my urge was all nonsense. The instant I put the thought from my mind Mr. Graham stopped his prayer and said to me: "Mrs. Mow, I have been resisting the urge to lay hands upon you and pray for you because I thought you might not understand it." That astounded me so I could not answer aloud. He came, laid hands on my head and prayed for me and I WAS RELEASED! No one can possibly know what that means unless they want God as much as I did and try to get over a seemingly impassable barrier as I did, and as many have. Just the absence of that awful long struggle is Peace to say nothing of what else there is to fill the empty space. *My fever was indeed gone in the great quiet of God.* It was too wonderful to feel ecstatic about . . .

The second night after this when we came down from the prayer room, a voice said in my right ear, "Don't take any pills tonight, I want to talk to you." (I had been taking soporific pills whenever on a strain at my doctor's direction, for I was not yet strong enough to go without sleep and the two nights before this I had taken some.) I thought that hearing voices belonged to psychical illusions. If this had happened before the coming of this freedom and quiet peace I would have thought that the strain of my struggle had caused this. But excitement was all gone. Anyway, this was so real that I obeyed and went to sleep at once.

At 2 a.m. I awoke—in the actual Presence of Jesus. And I was praying aloud as I awoke, saying: "Oh, Lord Jesus, come into my heart, come into my heart." There was a light in the corner of my bed. I mean a shining, definite Presence. I thought I must be dreaming and looked at my watch to verify my being awake. You've been in the Presence of God thus and you know how one cannot help but praise before Him, not the shouting kind, but the kind that makes one bow in adoration. The most wonderful thing to me was the realization of another Personality within me. The praying seemed to be entirely apart from me—it was another Spirit within. Then I realized the greatest lack

I had had before. I had been drawn and influenced by Christ, but there had not been enough of His Spirit within me to make full contact with the God without. I never realized that God within and without before . . . The fellowship of that sacred hour gave me an entirely new vision of prayer. I had never conceived the possibility of what was happening to me right then. Hearing a voice and seeing that divine Light there was not the outstanding thing—the most wonderful was the consciousness of the coming into my heart of a Presence. I am at an entire loss to describe what happened. *You* know and can understand; if you did not know, there would be no way of explaining it.

The Lord said to me: "Before this day is over I will baptize you with my Spirit . . ." After some time I got up and for an hour I read the Holy Spirit texts in the New Testament to try to find out what had happened to me. If I ever knew the Wesley teaching on the "second blessing" I did not remember it. Fragments of teaching from different ones now came to me but just what was Truth I wanted to know. John 13-17 were entirely new chapters to me now. I could now understand what Paul's great mystery and "Christ in me" meant. Everything had new meaning. I felt like searching the whole Word just then, as if I had just discovered a new gold mine—which I had. But after an hour I went to bed and to sleep. At five I awoke again, and this time had a like experience—I awoke praying: "The Fullness Lord, the Fullness, oh Lord, give me the Fullness." I never would have prayed that prayer before. I was afraid of that word Fullness for my exceedingly earthen vessel. Again He said: "This day you shall receive." And I answered in humility and adoration: "Behold Thy handmaid, be it unto me according to Thy word."

I think now that I know how Mary felt after the Holy Spirit overshadowed her. I had been overshadowed too, for His coming into my heart. The Lord said to me: "I will not stir *your* emotions, I will stir emotions in your heart." That statement has meant so much to me; even my good emotions are to be His, not mine. Looking at it in that light makes a difference. I am conscious daily in my contacts with others that I am "bound" to show His emotions. I had never found it hard to love most folks, but I found that I had had very little Christ-love. I told the Lord that I had wasted so many years and I wanted Him to send the fire to clean me up so I could fully serve Him to make up in a measure for the wasted years. I did not know what praying that meant. I have found out since ... Another thing he said to me that night was: "The reason you have stumbled so much and failed so long is because you have gone in your own strength. Go in my strength and you will not fail ..."

So, you see that no longer do I wonder about the personality of God. I understand the why of the after Resurrection appearances—He was there and then He wasn't. So they knew and I now know that whether I see Him or not, He *is*. I cannot thank Him enough for what He is to me. I only desire to be so like Him that others will want to know Him ... There is so much to learn, there is so much to do for Him, I only pray to be humble enough to be used, to go in His strength, so that my strength will be His and not be in the way. I want to be able to say with Paul: "But it is through the love of God that I am what I am, AND THE LOVE THAT HE SHOWED ME HAS NOT BEEN WASTED" (1 Cor. 15:10).

Since the night of her deeply moving confrontation with the Presence of Christ, Anna's outlook on life was from a totally different perspective. As she wrote later: "The old Anna had died." For two months she told no one what had happened, partly because it had been such an awesome and overwhelming experience that she could scarcely speak of it. Also, the memory of Russell Graham's words lingered with her: "If you have Christ in your heart your family will be the first to know." And they did. After two months she shared with Baxter what had taken place. Although his orientation was more scientific than of a mystical or spiritual nature, his devout religious faith made it possible for him to believe in and to fully accept this deeply revealing spiritual experience that had taken place in the life of his peppery and devout mate.

Anna was soon to discover that experiences of great ecstasy are frequently followed by feelings of despair and discouragement when one faces the fact that the same human weaknesses and faults are still present. One morning while walking in the hills near Landour she was thinking with chagrin about her own human frailty and the less desirable traits of her personality that were still with her, in spite of the fact that the living Presence had been made known to her. Suddenly, on the steep pathway going up the mountainside, she met an ancient and wizened little Indian woman who greeted her warmly and then said in some surprise: "How good it is to see you! I've been praying for you and the Lord gave me a special message that I should give you: 'Whenever we *see* we have failed it is evidence we are walking in the light.'"

So that was it!! The Presence had not made her perfect; it had not removed her ordinary everyday human emotions. It provided the light, the guidance, for her to see the changes that needed to be made and then she herself must do the necessary spiritual housecleaning. "That was the greatest spiritual lesson that I was ever given," asserted Sister Anna. Once again she realized that God's guidance comes at most unexpected times and via the most unexpected persons if we are only open to receive it.

The story of Anna's mystical confrontation with the divine Presence was never included in the thousands of speeches she made nor in any of the books she wrote. It was known by only a very, very few intimate persons with whom she had a deep spiritual bond. In the sharing of this experience she admitted quite frankly: "I've pushed some feelings back for so long I'm not sure I can talk about it." There were several reasons why she had a hesitancy about making it known. She never wanted anyone to believe that she had been "singled out" for any special spiritual favor. "What happened to me could happen to anyone," she emphasized. Her need was so great at that time in her life, her desire for a deeper relationship with God was so intense, that it may be the gift was given as an answer to the intense longing of her heart. Then, too, like her father before her who never wanted to be dressed so nicely that he could not identify with the poorest parishioner in the congregation, Anna felt that an experience such as this could be so overwhelming to some persons that it might serve to set her apart from their own struggling search after the Christlife.

She believed totally in the concept of *growth* in the Christian life and she never wanted people to believe that she saw herself as a finished product because of an overwhelming religious experience. This Christ revelation for her was not an end in itself but one step along the pathway to true spiritual maturity. Knowing herself as an impatient, quick-tempered, proud clay vessel, she knew it would be a lifelong process for her to make the Spirit *within* become completely alive in her relationship to the world *without*. She saw her baptism of the Holy Spirit as only a beginning. Like John Bunyan's Pilgrim, she realized that she as a person was only in process and that this holy happening was to be recognized for exactly what it was: a giant step along the Way.

Furthermore, Anna was wary of being connected with a great wave of emotionally-charged evangelism that had swept the western world during her childhood. Thousands of persons were "saved" in the sanctification and holiness movement that was a part of the religious picture at the end of the nineteenth century. The emotional impact was such that many persons were moved to experiences of great spiritual ecstasy that appeared to be only a surface glossing over of their real sins of the spirit. This kind of religiosity made very little difference in the living of their everyday lives.

Anna had been taught in the good Brethren tradition that the way a person lived, what she was at the center and core of her being, was what really mattered. This kind of teaching made her suspicious of religious experiences which had emotionally-inclined persons literally jumping over the church benches on Sunday mornings in fits of spiritual ecstasy while living like the devil the remainder of the week. There had been a lifetime of warning against the kind of religious experience that only tended to emphasize the "feeling" aspect. In Sister Anna's philosophy, people had to *be* good; they must be made over, transformed, their lives must reflect the image of the Christ they confessed.

There was another reason that emerged for her

reticence in making this story of her experience with the Presence generally known. It was so deeply moving to her at the time, so close to her heart, that she could scarcely speak of it without being moved to tears. There was deep emotion even after almost half a century had passed. There was no way such an awesome happening, such a deeply felt experience would fit into a speech. If those who were spiritually sensitive saw the result of what had happened, well and good. For others, all the telling in the world would not make it of value. The proof must be in her *living*, not in her *telling*.

What had taken place prepared her to face the remainder of her family's stay in India with a serenity she before would not have believed possible. It prepared her for facing the difficult "trial" which was held to determine whether she should be allowed to remain on the Indian mission field to complete their second term there. It prepared her for the months ahead in which she became more fully involved in the mission program with many added responsibilities. These were assumed with a physical strength as well as an emotional security that was not available to her heretofore.

In April of 1936, *The Fellowship*, a small newsletter for mission workers edited by E. Stanley Jones, carried an article written by Anna. There was one paragraph which indicated how deeply she felt about the change that had taken place in her life. She wrote:

> I feel a responsibility I never felt before. I am bound, gloriously bound, to see others with His eyes of love, to minister to others with His heart of love, to speak His words, smile His smile, and to partake of His sufferings. This coming of Him into my life was not only the end of a desperate search, but the beginning of a new life of faith in His service. And faith means *faith*, I find. In the life of faith God never builds bridges before us; He always builds them under our feet as we step forward in thin air!
>
> One great concern now is that I am not truly like Him in all my life. It takes me so long to grow into the fullness of His stature. But, whereas before I stumbled

in discouragement when I saw shortcomings and failure in my life, now I rejoice when my eyes are opened.

Anna's newly-found strength prepared her for the strain of getting her family of five ready to return to the United States in March 1940. It ultimately prepared her for facing the heart-hurting news that they would not be returned to the mission field when their second furlough had ended. Because of her close friendship with Madame Pandit and other Indian natives who were a part of the political movement that was stirring in India, the Mows found their name on a "black list" of persons who would not be allowed to return. No official visa would be issued to them. It was a blow. To be refused admission into the country which they had all come to love, the country which was "home" to their children, where they had many much-loved Indian friends, was painful. To a less hardy soul than Sister Anna it could have been devastating. By this time, however, she had come to rely so completely upon the hand of God in her life that this was just one more step by faith. If the door to India was closed, another would open. Of that she was sure.

And it did. During their furlough period she did some teaching at Bethany Theological Seminary where she had studied in previous years. When it became apparent that they could not return to India, a letter of invitation was extended to her by President Rufus D. Bowman asking her to become a member of the faculty at Bethany. Another venture of faith was about to begin, another phase of living in which she could put into practice those spiritual truths being revealed to her more clearly with the passing of each year. Her life was God's life, and because it was so it had to be good if lived within the context of His plans for her. In this, she lived, moved and was ready to further explore her being.

In reflecting on her India experience in later years Anna wrote:

> One of the things I learned in India was that one

can be very religious without being Christian. I was driven to find out what we had to contribute to those wonderful people. I found out in a new way about the wonder and grace of God. He wants me even more than I want him. It became spontaneous to respond to His love as revealed in the matchless love of Jesus my lord. Even growing in that love does not depend upon my own effort, only upon my choosing Him and accepting the power of His Holy Spirit. This makes a difference in my kitchen as well as in my church!

From the day of her experience in the Graham home, her belief in and dependence upon the Holy Spirit was the cornerstone of her Christian life and witness. She had found that "the Holy Spirit is not a substitute for an absent Lord but the agent of His Living Presence." She had met that Presence and from that day forward the impact could never be denied.

Chapter 4
The Joy of the Spirit

Sister Anna's years in India made a profound impact on her search for meaning in life. The spiritual serenity and security of some of the Indian people, many of whom lived lives of incredible economic hardship, forced her to reexamine some of the tenets of her own religious beliefs in a new light. She was by nature independent and self-sufficient and believed intensely in the rights of both men and women to develop their native gifts to their fullest potential.

She was surprised to discover, therefore, that the elderly Indian women, who in one sense had never had any "rights" at all, were treated like queens. Although the women of India had undergone much hardship and suffering, she found that they rarely felt sorry for themselves, seldom wallowed in the mire of self-pity which was sometimes characteristic of the women of her own native land. Their gentleness of spirit, their willingness to accept their lot in life with serenity challenged Anna, and she felt they had something to teach *her* about living. Sister Anna discovered "mutual mission" in India long before the term became a byword in modern mission efforts. She was bringing the good news of Christ to them, but they were teaching her to take a good, hard look at some of her own cherished concepts and beliefs.

From the mystics of the Eastern religions and the actions of their followers, she came to recognize that the source of their power and serenity was a spiritual strength that emanated from within their hearts. Surely there must be Something that her Christian faith had to offer that was comparable. This Something was discovered when she reached the end of her struggling search for a closer walk with God and yielded herself totally and completely to the Presence which was made known to her on that black, dark night in India in 1934. She found that it is only when we hunger spiritually that we receive the Holy Spirit, and the personal agony through which she was passing created that hunger to an intense degree. From that time forth she knew that the only thing that would truly satisfy her in life would be a personal, passionate devotion to the Person of Jesus Christ and to the values for which he lived and died.

Anna knew that God called no person merely to give an experience. He called persons to fulfill His long-range purposes in the unfolding drama of human history. Consequently, upon her return to a teaching position at Bethany Theological Seminary she determined to discover more of what the Holy Spirit was all about. She immediately plunged into some serious study which helped her to understand more clearly the role of the Holy Spirit in her own life as well as in the life of the church and of the world.

While living in India, she had come to appreciate the thinking and the spiritual depth of the great Indian mystic and poet, Sir Rabindranath Tagore. One of his haunting thoughts came to her as she attempted to understand the mysteries of the Christian faith which were beyond mere rational or intellectual explanation: "We are like a stray line from a poem," wrote Tagore, "which ever feels it rhymes with another and must find it or miss its fulfillment." St. Augustine had expressed much the same idea when he wrote: "O God, thou has made us for thyself and our hearts are restless until they rest in thee."

These stimulating ideas, her inquiring mind and her own mystical experience led her to do an intensive study of mysticism in religion. People of all nations, races and religions have had mystical experiences in the conventional understanding of the word. She felt it would be good to really know about some of their experiences and the results that were brought about in their lives.

Studying the lives of some of the Hindu mystics, as well as those of the early Christian mystics such as Polycarp, Clement, Origen, Plotinus, Ambrose, Augustine, Boniface and a number of others who followed in later centuries, she was led to recognize the importance of the "mystic experience" as one way God had of revealing His nature to His followers in the world. She came to see that God's way was a continuous process of creation and revelation, coming to those who were open to what He had to offer.

The paper she wrote as a result of her studies was entitled: *What is There in Mysticism for the Church of the Brethren?* One section is especially relevant. It is as fresh and important today as when written more than forty years ago. The Holy Spirit is not bound by time limits nor dependent upon the fads and techniques of a particular age nor a particular culture for its power.

> And what, in such a time as this, is there for the Church of the Brethren? Do we have a message? Is that message in an emphasis on one or two tenets on which our church was founded? Such as peace? Is it not deeper than that? The heart of the Pietist movement was deeper than one tenet. The Church of the Brethren was founded by an open mind on the New Testament. And not only by an open mind, but by a ready heart committed to follow whatever should be found in the Word. That is the very same as the commitment of Jesus to the Father's will. He never asked, "Will I do the Father's will?" That was a settled fact of his life. He asked only, "WHAT is my Father's will?" On that question and consecration was the Church of the Brethren founded.
>
> What church has such a modern approach? We are not bound with the creeds of other centuries, we have the original Message before us. We are not hampered or inhibited by the patterns of other men's experiences. We have the Christ before us. And we approach with an open mind and a ready heart if we are true "Dunkers."
>
> One of the most remarkable facts about the teaching of Jesus concerning the mystical life and the future Church is that he never gave any methods of finding and planning. By that very omission he tells us that the *Object* and not the *Method* is the important thing. When Jesus tried to prepare his disciples for his

leaving time, he said he had to go—so that the Holy Spirit would come. He was *with* them. The Holy Spirit was to be *in* them. As there was a mystical union between Him and the Father, so was there to be a mystical union between his followers and Him. Through the Holy Spirit He and the Father would dwell in the life of each Christian. This Holy Spirit would energize them, bring to mind things He had taught. (The Holy Spirit works where there is content but has nothing to get hold of in an empty mind.) The Holy Spirit would teach them new things and would guide them in new paths and in different circumstances. The Spirit would be a spring within the heart from which rivers of living water would flow to others. So the Christ-filled life cannot be selfish or secluded. Not, "What is coming to me," but what is flowing out. They were to wait for the coming of the Spirit, for if they went out in service before [the coming] they would be powerless.

In the study of the mystics and in the preparation of this paper, Anna pulled aside some of the "mythological drapery" from the writings of the early Christian saints and sifted out some of the extraneous material, preserving only those kernels of truth which would be important for her own growth. And those thousands of persons whom she reached through her ministries of teaching, preaching and writing were the beneficiaries of the continuing truth that had been revealed to her in a very special way.

Further study in church history under Dr. Floyd A. Mallott helped to broaden Anna's understanding of the importance of the Holy Spirit as the medium through which the church had survived down through the centuries. She concentrated on fourteen books concerning the lives of some of the early church fathers. The fresh air of heaven blew gustily through the pages of these books and Anna discovered that in the early Christian church the Spirit of God moved mightily. There was not yet the stifling truss of tradition to discourage action. There was not yet the over-organization and the over-emphasis on methods which came in later centuries to discourage creative individual initiative within the church as the Body of Christ. There was not time to seek security nor become complacent, because many of the early church leaders were "losing their heads," both literally and figuratively, for the privilege of following their newly discovered faith.

When someone wrote in later centuries that "the flower of Christianity never grew so rapidly as when watered by the blood of its martyrs," they probably were not aware that it was the Holy Spirit within the lives of the martyrs who provided them with the unshakable certainty against which persecution, imprisonment and death proved powerless. It had not yet become generally known that Christ's followers had that Something within them that was bigger than *anything* which could happen to them from the outside.

All these wonderful discoveries, and many more, came to Anna as she read and studied about the role of the Holy Spirit in the lives of the early Christian saints. She learned from Ignatius of Antioch that one should "test therefore by his works and his life the man who says he is inspired." She learned from Justin Martyr that one was not likely to receive the gift of the Holy Spirit unless the "thirst for truth" became one's predominating passion. Justin Martyr also pointed out that "real illumination is regeneration" and that what happened to a person after he had been filled was the real test, not just the mysterious process of the filling itself.

All of the early saints appeared to agree that central to the gift was the quality of love, the agape love which placed the well-being of another before one's own needs and desires. Such love, exemplified by Christ on the cross, appeared to be the only soil in which the Holy Spirit could mature and bear fruit once it had been planted in the life of the individual.

In another of her papers on mysticism, *The Mysticism of Paul the Apostle*, she wrote concerning the necessity of continuing growth as an imperative prerequisite for the life that would be open to God's gift of the Holy Spirit.

> No one who has received the new life from God lives sinfully because THE VERY NATURE OF GOD

DWELLS WITHIN HIM (1 John 3:9). Paul pleads with his converts to remember that they were Christ's, that they were dead to old things and must be alive to the things of Christ. They belonged to God, they were set apart for Him, had chosen Him. All this process of growth, made possible through Christ in the power of the Holy Spirit is really the process of sanctification—the process or rather the word so many Christians are afraid of. That is why so many are not growing, are not shedding the characteristics of the old man that still cling in the daily habits of life—because they do not see the necessity and privilege of this growing process . . . "Union with Christ" means the steady, unbroken glory of a quality of life which shines by its own light because it is essentially supernatural, allows no hint of any negative, because the very "fullness of God" is in it. It is becoming like Christ, through the Spirit of Christ given in the heart by faith, which works from the inside out into every phase of life. *If love is not there, the Spirit is not there.*

Because of her own mystical experience in India and because of her years of studying the lives of those who had kept the church alive through the centuries, Anna became a recognized advocate of the need for and the power of the Holy Spirit in the Christian church in the latter part of the twentieth century. This was not only true for her own denomination, the Church of the Brethren, but it was true for the church at large. The Holy Spirit recognizes no denominational lines nor creeds. The Spirit supercedes all the manmade barriers that have been created through the years to stifle the progress of God at work in the world. Through the medium of the Holy Spirit, Anna saw God continuing His divine purposes, and nothing gave her greater joy than to proclaim His presence to all who would listen.

> A church that has a special dip in baptism for the Holy Spirit should be the most experienced in the function and effectiveness of the Holy Spirit, but I am afraid that our historic emphasis on the "good life" weaned us away from the essential importance of the Spirit for a true life of God,

warned Sister Anna as she stood before the delegate body of the 1972 Annual Conference of the Church of the Brethren.

> We were baptized in the name of the Father, the Son and the Holy Spirit. Then we looked to the New Testament for guidance, to know God's will for us. Theologies, ordinances, doctrines and customs developed but they have always been open-ended because of our type of organization. The question before us today is: What is the guidance of the Spirit in an everchanging culture? . . . It is a fact not always recognized that the delegates to Annual Conference have more power in the policies of our church than anyone at our so-called church headquarters at Elgin. You delegates on this floor must be under the full guidance of the Holy Spirit so that the church people will not be confused.

That the "church people" of all denominations were confused in the mid-decades of the 20th century is an indisputable fact. Thousands of persons were leaving the more traditionally oriented Protestant faiths to become members of rapidly growing "independent" churches which were often centered on the charisma of an individual human leader rather than on the hard teachings of Jesus Christ. Thousands more were turning to the radio and television ministries for their spiritual food, becoming less and less involved with local congregations of believers. Thousands of youth and many intellectually-inclined adults were finding their spiritual succor in cults such as Scientology, in the meditative movements and in the Eastern religions which were springing up in the Western world like mushrooms in the loam of restless yearning caused by religious discontent.

Divisions within many well-established denominations and local congregations of Christians were not uncommon. There was much fuel to nourish the fires of malcontent that were smoking. There was the question of accepting contemporary worship forms and music; there was the eternal struggle to determine whether people were worshiping *tradition* or *truth*; there was the role of the church in relation to the political scene; there was the race issue which affected the membership structure of old, well-established congregations in the inner city, created fears about property values, changing work roles, changing school systems and the thorny issue of interracial marriages. There was the question of the role of women in the church, and the changing family structure which cultural and economic changes were bringing about. A Christ-centered commitment toward problems relating to human sexuality was causing a re-examination of the issue of abortion and of both heterosexual and homosexual lifestyles.

Cultural changes due to technical discoveries and economic changes brought about conflicting "lifestyle" values between generations. The mechanization and computerization of daily life and entertainment had so depersonalized the routine aspects of living that the fine art of human relations seemed secondary in the scheme of life. The hardened acceptance of violence and crime as a fact of life had created a mood of fear that hovered over the world like a dark, black cloud ready to empty its poisoned contents on the hapless victims beneath its shadow. The assassination and the attempted assassinations of numerous world leaders left the world in a state of disbelief that we had degenerated to this depth.

Two more black clouds hung over a stricken world: the threat of worldwide starvation because of the misuse and abuse of the spaceship-earth's natural resources and environment, and the all too awesome possibility of the annihilation of humankind through nuclear warfare. The mushroom cloud which had risen from the Nevada desert when the first atomic bomb was exploded had now, figuratively speaking, spread its poisoned possibilities throughout the entire world. The pain engendered by worldwide warfare pervaded the international atmosphere like the smothering penetration of a blanket of heat on a hot, muggy August afternoon. A kind of ironic climax came with the struggle between the British Empire and Argentina over some rocky, jagged islands so small they were almost dwarfed by the monstrous war machines that rushed to their "defense" from thousands of miles away. It almost appeared that homo sapiens had gone utterly berserk in the management of His domain for which the Lord God had established such high hopes.

Out of the black hopelessness that hovered over the earth's peoples, however, there began to be a rising crescendo for a return to sanity, and the plea that peaceful negotiations replace armed force in the resolution of international problems. The numerous peace movements throughout the world in the early eighties brought together an interesting assortment of "bedfellows." There were the remnants of the "flower children" of the fifties and sixties. A limited number of politicians were more interested in saving the human race than salvaging a few votes. There were the realistic economists and environmentalists who saw the futility of destroying the earth's resources in defense of the political pride and paternalistic power grabbing of world leaders who had not yet caught up with the fact that we live in an interdependent age which simply does not allow the luxury of self-centered nationalism.

There were the idealistic youth of the world who only wanted to live and let live. And there were the women of the world, their mothers, who had always suffered the most from the effects of war. There were the so-called peace churches who had always declared that war is morally wrong and spiritually devastating. There were members of the medical profession who pointed out that the idea of salvaging enough equipment and personnel to take care of the wounded following a nuclear holocaust was a sheer pipedream. There was a large contingent of scientists who, perhaps better than all the rest, realized that this instrument which had been brought into being was now out of hand. At long last, the realists, the pragmatists of the earth began to join with the poets, the prophets and the philosophers to declare that mankind's foolishness in using war as a means of international problem resolution had gone far enough.

It was into this maelstrom of contemporary confusion that Sister Anna brought her clarion call for a return to the voice of the Holy Spirit as the one and only safe guide for the welfare of individuals and of the church as the Body of Christ within the world. The search for the mind of Christ in a confused world left many Christians bewildered, however. Those who were not deeply rooted in the history of the Christian faith often found themselves being emotionally swayed by this or that "man of God" who had some very simplistic answers to some very complex problems. Anna had a genuine fear of those who would use emotional means as a tool to gain selfish ends, even in the church. She believed deeply in the right kind of emotion but never in manipulated emotion.

Putting God at the center, not one's personal *feelings*, was the course she felt must be followed in achieving a spiritual high. "Sometimes," she wrote, "men take advantage of people's desire for emotional satisfaction and cash in on it, not to lead men to God, but to gain for themselves excellent reports and prestige. How many millions have missed the way and been short-circuited in their sincere search for God because the "church" has been more concerned with its own prestige and power than in giving honor to God!" Power, God's power, is to be used *for* people, not *over* them in Sister Anna's scheme of spiritual growth. She often has told the story of a woman who once asked her: "Why don't I have the Holy Spirit?" Anna answered her: "Well, the Spirit is power, dynamo, dynamite. If you had power what would you do with it?" The woman thought for a moment and then, out of her real concern for the church she declared: "If I had the power! If I had the power I would get rid of all the people in the church that are blocking its progress." Sister Anna promptly answered: "That is exactly why God does not give you power. He wants you to win all those problem people!"

One of the most important roles Anna has filled during her later years is that of serving as a "reconciler" between groups causing dissension within local congregations. Numerous church fellowships had problems stemming from a divided membership because of the growing emphasis on what is loosely called the "charismatic movement." Into these churches she is often invited because she is able to sit down with each of the dissenting groups, hear them out and in some cases bring them back together again in true Christian fellowship. When she has been invited to serve as a mediator between persons with intense feelings about their positions of right or left, her winsomeness and nonmanipulative approach was in most cases successful.

Anna is devoted to calling forth the best in others, has a sound knowledge of the psychological process and no fear about calling a spade a spade when this is necessary. She comes across as a caring colleague in the search for wholeness, and there were very few times when she has failed to effect growth—growth for individual persons as well as for divided congregations. She was especially a bridge over troubled waters in the sixties and seventies. While many were pointing to dogmas and doctrines, she pointed to a Person and His way of life as the solution to personal as well as corporate problems. Genie Price wrote of her own personal experience in learning to understand the role of the Holy Spirit as interpreted by Anna:

> I have had little confusion, few recurring doubts, no uneasiness over the mystery of the Holy Spirit's work and Presence in human life and there is a specific reason why I have not: For most of the years in which I have followed Jesus Christ, I have known and listened to Anna Mow. In all honesty, I can tell you that I have read no books, heard no sermons, no teaching which more clearly delineated in down to earth, understandable language the enormous potential of the indwelt life... She is a peacemaker, among Christians in particular. Many of us would like to be just that, but Anna's facile mind, her ageless insights, her own Spirit-guided daily life give her a Divine "hand up" in this often prickly work. Dogmatic, varying viewpoints on the time of coming, the duration of the stay, the actual work of the Holy Spirit have divided Christians to a degree that causes me to sit and wonder. Because of what I have learned from Anna, I am certain that there is no need for such divisiveness, because God Himself is not divided and His Spirit—if understood at all clearly—will keep us posted as to God's nature and His eternal commitment to us all.

One of Anna's strongest beliefs is that the Holy Spirit is in the world for the purpose of uniting us, not dividing us. In a message to a group of ministers from many denominations she stated:

> The often-quoted comments of the early apostles about the gifts and fruits of the Spirit have too often been used to divide the union of Christendom. The problem is not in the Spirit but in the way human beings insist on imposing their own spiritual experiences on others rather than trusting God to manifest Himself in appropriate ways to all his creation. Sometimes I see love being used as a hammer. In the personal relationship which the person-seeking God comes to have with him, the Spirit continually expands its power. This has little to do with reciting personal experiences about an encounter with Christ if a similar experience is expected from others.

Dr. James Stewart of Scotland was one of the most ardent advocates of the strength and power that was to be found through the Holy Spirit in the lives of individuals and of the church as the body of Christ. At the conclusion of her 1972 Annual Conference address Anna quoted from Dr. Stewart's book, *The Wind of the Spirit*:

> Don't try to tame that intractable wind. No act of convocation or assembly can circumscribe it, no political dictator curb it, no rooted personal prejudice block it . . . And don't you see? This is the essential optimism of Christianity. Here in the Spirit of Christ is a force capable of bursting into the hardest paganism, discomfitting the most rigid dogmatism, electrifying the most suffocating ecclesiasticism. This is the sovereign freedom of the Holy Spirit. There is no citadel of self and sin that is safe from Him, no unbelieving cynic secure beyond His reach. There is no ironclad bastion of theological self-confidence that is immune, no impregnable agnosticism He cannot disturb into faith, no ancient ecclesiastical animosities He cannot reconcile. And blessed be His name, there is no winter death of the soul that He cannot quicken in-

to a blossoming springtime of life, no dry bones He cannot revitalize into a marching army. This is the glory of Pentecost.

And this was Sister Anna's glory: that she might bear witness faithfully and forever to the joy the Spirit had brought to her own life—that she in turn might bring glory to God.

Chapter 5

Wisdom, the World and Holy Hilarity

The impact of Sister Anna as a teacher at Bethany Theological Seminary between the years of 1941 and 1958 will be felt for generations. She served as an instructor in several areas: Christian education, home and family life, personal devotional life and other courses relating to the basics of Christian living. Kahlil Gibran must have had in mind a teacher like her when he wrote: "The teacher who walks in the shadow of the temple among his followers, gives not of his wisdom but rather of his faith and his lovingness." It was this faith and lovingness that made such an impact on her students.

True, she had the appropriate academic background for teaching; she had years of rich living and practical experience on which to draw. But over and above all this, her mystical experience in India had convinced her that it was only to the degree in which she had the "Christ within" that she could make Him available to her students. Not until the "inner Anna" and the "outer Anna" were one and the same would she be most effective. It wasn't her knowledge nor her teaching style that were most important; it was her lifestyle, her reflection of Him to Whom she was totally dedicated. This was what made her a teacher never-to-be-forgotten.

During the Bethany years her life also touched the lives of hundreds of persons who were in no way connected with the school. Her love for the people of India led her to become a member of an organization which was founded to promote better understanding between the Eastern and Western cultures. Soon the Mow apartment was literally a home away from home for dozens of foreign students from the International House in Chicago. An enthusiastic guest once declared it to be "one of the few places in Chicago with an international atmosphere." Students, journalists, businessmen, poets, scientists, writers, foreign political figures—people from many walks of life and from many different countries came to share in a meal of Anna's famous curry and rice or simply to have tea. And always along with the food for their bodies was the water of life for their souls.

One of their most frequent visitors was Tarini Prasad Sinha, an assistant professor of Political Science at Roosevelt College. After his death in 1946, Anna wrote: "Mr. Sinha has left many footprints on our floor. He was ever more than a guest. He had a genius for being one of the family wherever he went... He has left more memories in the kitchen than in any other room. There are no dishes that he has not washed. There are many pungent spices which he brought to concoct some delectable Indian dish. The memories of his cooking and his ability to be host in another's kitchen are heartwarming indeed." And for Mr. Sinha it was "heartwarming indeed" that he had the freedom to be a host in Anna's kitchen.

The Mow guest books for these seventeen years read like an international roster of Who's Who in Chicago. In addition to India, visitors came from Germany, Japan, China, Puerto Rico, Paraguay, Africa, England, Lebanon and the Philippines. On New Year's Eve, 1945, the Mows' spiritual brother, E. Stanley Jones, was a guest along with a number of other friends. One of them wrote in their book that evening: "Lo! here is fellowship!" Others throughout the years echoed similar sentiments. "Here we meet as citizens of the world," wrote one. Another: "The times are back in joint, curry and rice—wonderful." Their home was a sanctuary for many, many lonely hearts.

Rosa Page Welch, the famous Black singer, became a close friend and her name appeared as a guest on numerous occasions. When the Mows left Chicago she wrote: "I am thankful for the magnificent way God has used and worked through you to teach and give guidance and help in molding the lives of so many, many people all around His great big, wonderful world! And I am one of those many people. Our Lord has given me many wonderful friends but no one has made a greater contribution to my life in so many ways . . . You've opened the way for me to meet many fine people of other races and nationalities in your cozy home, overflowing with warmth and love in Christian fellowship for all of God's children."

Another guest during those years was Vijaya Lakshmi Pandit, one of Anna's dearest Indian friends. At that time she was serving as India's Ambassador to the United States. She had been told by Washington authorities that she should not stop in Chicago until she had first come to Washington. "She stopped anyway," laughed Anna, "because she was not bound by protocol or anything else so superficial. She had a freedom that prestige-conscious people know nothing about." The Mows had a small dinner party for Madame Pandit while she was in Chicago, and a guest asked Anna: "How did *you* ever learn to know *her*?" The tension was removed from the very pointed question when Anna replied with great glee: "Oh, I learned to know her when she was a jailbird." The fact that it was a true story made it all the better.

During the days Madame Pandit was in Washington as Ambassador she once said to Anna: "Oh, Anna, it was so much easier in our jail days; then the issues were all black and white. In Washington too many issues are all gray." "But," said Anna, "she had learned to see through the gray of national and world politics because she never lost her vision of freedom, justice and peace for all." She continued to think of others, not of herself, when she became India's Minister of Health and was subsequently to serve in the positions of Governor, Ambassador to Russia and the United States as well as the first woman president of the United Nations. Madame Pandit was the recipient of nine honorary degrees besides other untold honors.

It was one of those beautiful accidents of history that brought these two remarkable women into each other's lives. Not only was there a personal affection for each other but their families were also involved. Anna was asked to look after the three Pandit daughters while they were attending college in the United States, and once while their mother was in the hospital for an operation Anna stayed with the girls for three weeks in New York. Lekha, the middle daughter, declared impulsively one day: "We love you, Sister Anna, because you adore Mummy just like we do." It was a mutual love. Madame Pandit wrote in later years: "Anna Mow is perhaps my dearest foreign friend. I have gained enormously by her friendship and have been sustained by her love. I've also learned a little humility from her."

In addition to the steady stream of visitors during the Bethany years, there were dozens of family members who came to call. For two of those years Anna's mother was with her. Completely bedfast, she received the love and care she so needed from the entire Mow family. "Although my mother could no longer speak because of her stroke," said Anna, "she was a true blessing to our home. The students used to come to 'cheer her up' with a visit—but they always went away having been cheered themselves because of Mother's warm smile and radiant spirit."

There was another facet of service during Anna's Chicago years. She was a member of the Joint Department of Evangelism for the National Council of Churches of Christ in America (NCCCA). In this capacity she spoke in many churches in the Chicago area and participated in numerous Christian Missions held at various universities and colleges in the Midwest. She was also a frequent speaker at the United Christian Youth Missions. It was during this period that Dr. Jesse M. Bader, Executive Director for the NCCCA, became a warm personal friend and an ardent admirer of her contribution to the ecumenical activity of God's people in His world. Upon her retirement from the seminary in 1958 he wrote: "You have poured your mind and heart without reservation into students who are to be the leaders in the Kingdom tomorrow... The good Lord endowed you with so many talents. I never saw anyone who could do so many things and do them so well. These abilities range all the way from cooking Indian curry to preaching a sermon..."

Dr. Nels Ferré, Abbot Professor of Christian Theology at Andover Newton Theological School, was another friend who deeply appreciated the ministry Anna brought to him during a very trying period of his life. "What a privilege it is for me to be included among those who wish you well," wrote Dr. Ferré. "For many years now, I have felt you to be the best kind of friend. The fact that you have told me that you carry me and my work on your prayer list has humbled me and made me ever more deeply desirous to offer up my life more fully to God for Christian witness and service. Ever so often I have been cheered by the thought of your personality and your friendship and the kind of faith that I know to be real."

The years in Chicago also saw the beginning of her lifelong involvement with the Christian Ashram movement in America. Her friendship in India with E. Stanley Jones and her participation in the Ashram movement there convinced her that there was a real need for such a "spiritual retreat" movement in America. When Jones returned to America from India it was only natural that he would turn to Sister Anna for help in getting this movement started in America. (The Ashram work in America is fully covered in Chapter 8.)

Another of her ecumenical involvements was her work with the School of Leadership Education for the Church Federation of Greater Chicago. Here she taught classes in Christian education, and her thorough knowledge of child psychology, her natural love for children and her own unique style of teaching made her a much sought after person in this important field. She was also involved in the Chicago Missionary Institute, sponsored by the Council of Church Women of Greater Chicago. She participated in numerous Bible Institutes sponsored by various interdenominational groups. She preached frequently at the Chinese Christian Church Union of Chicago and she worked in a Japanese Prison Camp where she served those who had been imprisoned by the American government at the outbreak of World War II. All of these activities were in addition to her full teaching load at Bethany, including her service often as the seminary's "unofficial" hostess, and her looking after the needs of her mother and three teenage children.

The Chicago years demanded a lot of hard work, but they also brought Anna a bonus: the opportunity to indulge in her love for the beautiful in life. Next to her love for God and His people was her love for the arts: music, painting, sculpture. There were numerous art galleries, an outstanding symphony, and several opera companies in Chicago. Although both time and money were limited, Anna bought a season ticket for the opera and symphony programs and the entire family took turns using it. This investment paid off well because all three of her children are accomplished musicians. Their preliminary music training in the Mission School at Landour, India, had prepared them well to fully appreciate the musical experiences available in Chicago. Stealing an hour or two every few weeks to have her soul refreshed by great music, great drama and great paintings was one of the ways Anna was able to maintain her equilibrium in a schedule that was so demanding. She understood the importance of taking time to smell the flowers along life's way. Doing this she not only enriched her own life and the lives of her children but she also prepared herself for the coming years. She would have the enjoyment of listening to her beloved music on the radio and records if and when she was forced to be less active because of illness or advancing age. How wise she was!

Upon her retirement from teaching in 1958, she was presented with a book of letters from grateful students, faculty members and other friends. Letters from her students revealed clearly their depth of affection for her. Verbatim quotations from some of these give insight into those aspects that made her such an able teacher. A Methodist pastor who had been a former student wrote: "Because your teaching comes not just from books but even more from the heart, your teaching will never stop as long as you have any kind of contact with people anywhere." A similar thought was echoed by another: "You show that you are a letter from Christ... You write not with ink but with the Spirit of the living God, not on tablets of stone, but on tablets of human hearts." Another: "Your life has cleared my vision of God's son; you've brought friendliness to the lonely, courage to the disheartened, faith to the confused, hope to the despairing."

A former Mennonite student wrote: "Your penetrating, sometimes piercing probing of our spirit with the Spirit whom you know and love—this was like opening windows to let fresh air into stuffy rooms crowded with theological furniture. Keep opening windows!" Another shared: "The academic is needed, but the living Spirit of true devotional life must always be present to give power and purpose to that which we learn. We felt this emphasis in all your classes and I want to thank you for the help it has given and is still giving."

Numerous others wrote in the same vein, but probably the one which most warmed her heart came from her only brother, William H. Beahm. He had served as dean of the seminary during part of her tenure there. He wrote: "We are grateful for your generosity in friendship, for your unfailing confidence and good cheer, and for your constant emphasis upon the life of the Spirit of God in the hearts of His children. You have been devoted without stint and devotional without cant. It has been a joy to be your colleague for nearly two decades." In closing his warm and loving letter, William spoke of the hospitality in Anna's home and the informing conversation, intriguing comment and ready interest that had always been available to him and his wife Esther from both Sister Anna and her husband, Baxter.

Many of the letters reflected the ecumenical aspect and the cosmopolitan atmosphere which the Mow family had brought to the Bethany campus. This was partly a result of her years in India, but surely the "window on the world" aspect of her childhood also played a part in making it so. Eddie Asivatham, one of the Indian students who frequently spent time in Anna's home, wrote: "You are one of the few that I have known who have been able to hold together your loyalty to your own country and the country which you served for so many years . . . This you were able to do by reconciling the two together in the larger loyalty to the Kingdom." Dr. Norman J. Baugher, the late General Secretary of the Church of the Brethren, expressed the appreciation of the entire church as the body of Christ when he wrote: "Of inspiration to many of us has been your ecumenical spirit and involvement. You have loved the whole church of Jesus Christ while loving the Church of the Brethren. We thank you for demonstrating in our midst an inclusiveness that joins arms with all Christians."

Without a doubt, Anna raised the spiritual sights of hundreds of students and friends. She helped them to see that the members of God's family would find their way to Him by many and diverse pathways.

One of Anna's great assets as a teacher was her deep, spiritual sensitivity to those who needed encouragement. Her teaching extended far outside the classroom. It entered into the very lives of the students no matter where they happened to meet. There were frequent references in their letters to chance conversations that took place in the grocery store, on a street corner, in the warm atmosphere of her always open home. Somehow her sensitive spiritual antenna always seemed to be in operation in order that she might pick up on a person's need at exactly the right moment.

A fellow staff member wrote gratefully: "Your hastily penned words on a Christmas card served as an encouragement to me at a time when I needed it, and I thought no one knew. But you did! You must have known somehow that these were the right words to say at that precise moment." Many persons, students and others were benefactors of her intuitive understanding of their needs. One student wrote: "As near as I can define it, it's what Christlikeness must be. It is a deep quality which radiates intangible feelings of deep understanding and compassionate sympathy and genuine spiritual love . . . I received something in your class and in our Indian fellowship dinner that smacked of the warmth and encouragement of Jesus himself."

Her awareness of pain in others was acute, and if she sometimes unwittingly caused pain to another it was a devastating experience for her. Once in a jesting mood she had asked a shy new student if he was acting as the "devil's advocate." The young man, never having heard that expression before, believed she was accusing him of acting like the devil. It was not until weeks later that she began to discover the many painful experiences of his childhood and how he had been called a "little devil" enough times to give him a deep complex about the title. Through reassurance and encouragement from Anna, then as well as in later years, he came to know that her caring for him was so deep that she was wounded far more than he by the unintentional name calling. So deeply, in fact, that when she repeated this story many decades later there were tears in her eyes for the pain she had caused.

There was a simplicity and sound common sense in her teaching that made a lasting impression on her students. "I guess the thing that attracted me to you was that I could feel your love toward all," wrote one frank student, "and that although you knew what you were talking about you still made me feel at ease and like you were just another person like everyone else. So often teachers seemed in some other realm." One of her men students commented: "You have been blessed with an uncommon amount of common sense. This, combined with your deep commitment to Christ and daily companionship with Him reveals why you are so eagerly sought out as a friend and counselor in any group in which you move." Another student, trying to analyze his own feelings about her teaching, wrote: "You had the coveted grace of coupling wisdom with experience. You made the profoundest ideas in books seem as mere illustrations of what you had already discovered in practical experiences of life . . . To you the trivial remarks of a student often seemed funny. And yet when a truth was defended or a point was to be made, it was spewed out like the venom of a coiled rattlesnake . . . You sometimes displayed a bluntness that was void of all grace. I once read a paper in class and had no more than read three sentences when the sound of a Dunker's 'Amen!' interrupted the process as though all conclusions were evident in the introduction!"

Along with her sagacious wisdom there was her "holy hilarity" which endeared her to so many. These two traits are seldom, if ever, so splendidly blended in one person. Half of the two hundred or more letters mentioned her keen sense of humor as being one of her most effective teaching tools. There was that radiant, overflowing joy coming out frequently in flashing bits of humor followed by her characteristic cackle. "Is that lady who laughs like a chicken leaving Bethany?" asked one small child when he heard his parents discussing Anna's impending departure. Along with this little boy many others knew that things would never be quite the same around the campus without her infectious good humor. "Since knowing you I'm sure God has a good hearty laugh," one student wrote. And another assured her that, "Knowing a Christian who could live a saint's life and laugh at any and everything has given me a wonderful lift. You make me sure that Christ enjoyed a cute joke occasionally Himself! God invented laughter as surely as He did tears or sorrow. Your 'holy hilarity' has made me sure of this."

No letter caught the spirit of Anna as a teacher so well as one from a fellow professor who had observed her work for many years. Dr. Jesse Zeigler, director of counseling services at the school, commented on her refreshing spontaneity and rare sense of humor and wisdom. He closed his letter with: "It is truly refreshing and wholesome to find a person who speaks and acts spontaneously without always giving the impression of having thought through what the political implications of a particular word or move may be . . . The depth of your spiritual insight is great, yet devoid of the kind of snobbery which sometimes makes spiritual insight unacceptable. Your last chapel address contained many gems of insight yet it seemed to be completely devoid of pretentiousness. This is a rare gift."

Anna was also a true scholar. This was evidenced in many ways. First, there was her dedication to growth, to the continuing quest for knowledge. The fact that she earned two degrees during the years she also carried a full teaching load was indicative of her belief that the learning process was never a finished one. She was a student of the Bible, of the classics, of life itself. She tried to learn something from every person she ever met, every happening to which she was exposed. Into her ninetieth year she had a sharpness of recall that was amazing. Her knowledge of current books, television programs and the current political scene was astounding. Once when discussing her reading habits she casually remarked that she still read several current theological journals regularly. "Because," she stated good-naturedly, "I have to keep up with the fellows I taught years ago. I have to know what they're being exposed to today!"

She continued reading books by the dozens until an eye operation curtailed that. For all too many persons the end of formal schooling also means the end of real study. Anna recognized that education only gives one the tools for learning, the *real* education takes place in the school of life, in the lifelong process of becoming. Life with her was seen as process, not merely as means to an end. And since life is a continuing process the real scholar recognizes and acts on the need for continuing study.

A second scholarly hallmark was her willingness to travel the second mile in pursuit of factual information on a subject. It was interesting to note the bibliography of her graduate research papers. Where four or five books were required reading she would have read those plus at least a half dozen more. Most of her papers were marked with an "A" by her professors and each indicated a thorough knowledge of the subject. Much of the information in her papers is as pertinent today as when written over forty years ago. Such timelessness is another indication of scholarly writing.

A third demonstration of her scholarship was her capacity for making the profound simple. She could, and did, read numerous complicated theological treatises, extract the information that was most pertinent and then translate it into language that could be understood by anyone. She had the capacity for getting at the kernel of basic truth in what she read and letting the extraneous matter fall by the wayside. The facts put down in her own distinctive fashion after being sifted through that facile brain made fascinating reading. Her books, lectures and articles were all done in a way that could be understood by anyone who was willing to listen with an open mind and a reasonable degree of attentiveness. What she said and wrote was simple but it was not simplistic. It bore the stamp of one who knew where she came from, who knew where she was going and to Whom she belonged. It came from the heart; it went to the heart.

Finally, one of the more significant marks of Anna's scholarship was the well-developed faculty for discernment of what was *real* and what was *pseudo*. The real scholar recognizes and gives tribute to that which is beyond himself; the pseudo scholar too often says: "Behold, look at what I have wrought!" The real scholar studies and writes to bring light to a subject; all too often the pseudo scholar studies and writes to impress other scholars. Although Anna could hold her own in any deep theological or academic discussion, she had absolutely no need for parading either her intellectual capacity or the degrees that followed her name. With her, knowledge was not something to be displayed like fine jewelry or expensive possessions. Knowledge was to help one understand other human beings, to help one to live better. Learning merely for the sake of learning was not enough. It must be used to advance the cause of Him whom she served. It was as simple as that. Sister Anna was a scholar, a pedant she was not.

The years dedicated to the development of her intellectual gifts brought their rewards. There was the deep satisfaction resulting from the pursuit of excellence in the use of her own native capabilities. There was the rich reward of friendships made while studying and teaching with persons of like mind—persons who, like herself, recognized that wealth of mind and spirit was the true wealth. There were the tangible rewards: seven degrees, four earned and three honorary. The earned degrees covered a span of more than 25 years and were earned from Manchester College, B.A., 1918; and Bethany Theological Seminary, B.D., 1921, M.R.E., 1941, M.T., 1943. Those conferred as honorary came from Bethany Theological Seminary, D.D., 1976; Elizabethtown College, D.L., 1975; Manchester College, D.D., 1976. It is doubtful if seven academic degrees ever sat so appropriately and yet so lightly upon the head of the one so honored.

The honorary degree conferred by Elizabethtown College was an especially significant one for her because of the fact that her father had served as president of the college in her early childhood and also because the second honorary degree was conferred that day upon a young artist of such ability and such charm that Anna was to say later: "He just made the day for me!" The artist was Jimmy Wyeth, internationally known in his own right, son of Andrew Wyeth, one of America's best-known and loved artists. In reporting on the occasion, a newspaper reporter wrote: "While the diminutive Mrs. Mow, holder of four earned degrees and one other honorary one, participated in the proceedings with an experienced air, Wyeth studied his first college commencement with a bemused smile. 'It's all very strange for me,' he said, in an interview before the commencement. 'It's very new because I never went to college!'" A personal note sent to Anna after this occasion indicated that it had been a mutually inspiring and fun occasion for him. Getting to know *her* had made *his* day.

Chapter 6
Surrender

Time is humanity's great common denominator, the only possession of which we all have equal amounts. Some persons merely drift with the times and tides of life, asking for little, contributing less. Others appear to exist with purpose, living in a way that leaves definite marks on the drama of human history either for good or for evil. The question is not how they do so, but why. Their credo is of primary importance; what they live *for* is what matters most. The how, the methodology by which they achieve their ends, is secondary.

Anna was one of those who began early in life to cherish idealistic thoughts about making one's life count for good. In childhood, the deep faith of her parents instilled a reverence and love for her Creator. Life was a gift, a gift one should use "for the glory of God and the good of one's neighbor." Life was for intentional living, not for dreaming and drifting. Life was for commitment, the return of one's resources, time and energy to the One to whom one belonged. She was God's person and as such the primary reason for existence was to reflect His love to the world, to give to His other children the rich spiritual gifts which had been given to her.

Such aspirations are not arrived at instantaneously. At the age of 18, her strong sense of commitment for service on the mission field was indicative of the fact that she was ready to live life on God's terms and not on her own. Her subsequent service in India was filled with a mixture of experiences: joy at the birth of three children; deep emotional pain because of misunderstood motivations; the continuing discovery of devout religious faiths and worthwhile social mores differing from the ones to which she had heretofore been exposed. Finally, there was the agonizing spiritual searching for that Something beyond herself to which she could turn for guidance and comfort in times of stress.

Although she was a serious student she did not give a lot of thought to the development of a creed for living out her life until her return to the Bethany campus as a teacher in 1942. Her encounters with the mystical religions of the Eastern culture, her participation in the Indian Christian Ashram Movement, and her own mystical experience made her eager to learn more of the lives of those who had made an impact on the world because of their religious beliefs and actions.

This interest led to the reading of dozens of books, attendance at numerous lectures and the ultimate writing of several scholarly papers. At this stage in life she no longer sought knowledge merely for the sake of knowledge. Neither was it sought only to earn additional academic degrees. It was sought with the objective of discerning more clearly the direction her own life should take. She wanted to give a more adequate response to the calls of the church. But most of all she wanted to respond more fully to the challenge of discovering the "mind of Christ" for her own life.

Three of her papers, *What is There in Mysticism for the Church of the Brethren?*, *Pharisaism and Legalism*, and *The Contribution of the Church Fathers to the Spiritual Life of the Church*, not only helped to earn two graduate degrees but they tended to greatly enlarge her vision of God's role in relation to humankind. Graduate studies in the books of the Old and New Testaments further enhanced her growing appreciation for the ways God fulfilled His purposes in the world through such mere mortals as King David and Saints Peter, Paul and John. In her speaking and teaching Anna often emphasized with her familiar chuckle that "God had to knock Paul down to get him, but He got him!" It was out of this intensive study of the saints of past centuries that her own credo for living began to take shape.

Anna believed in a *surrendered life*, a life of servanthood, a life lived totally within the context of the Father's will. But it had to be total surrender. No halfway measures were enough. In an address to the 1949 Church of the Brethren Annual Conference, she stated: "One of the most devastating things we can do to those who want to follow the Lord is to let them get the idea that they can be partially consecrated. Actually it is psychologically and spiritually impossible to be half surrendered to God ... Surrender is without reservation or it is not surrender."

Her own life was greatly influenced by the lives of the early church fathers about whom she had studied. From them she learned that it was a rare soul who was willing to go *all* the way in surrender to God. According to one, Meister Eckhart: "There are plenty of people to follow our Lord halfway, but not the other half. They will give up possessions, friends and honors, but it touches them too closely to disown themselves ... Only now and then comes a man or a woman who is willing to be utterly obedient, to go the other half, and to follow God's faintest whisper. But when such a commitment comes in a human life, God breaks through, miracles are wrought, world-renewing divine forces are released, history changes."

Both Sister Anna and Meister Eckhart had valid reason for their belief in the necessity for a totally surrendered life. It was the example of Jesus himself. "Not my will but Thine be done" was His prayer in the most agonizing moment of His life. So must ours be. If it was necessary for Him to go to the cross in order to fulfill the divine purposes for which His life was intended, might it not also be necessary at times for His followers to do the same? Anna was always ready to point out, however, that Jesus' cross was *chosen*; it was not imposed upon Him. He *chose* to be obedient to His Father, and it was obedience born of love, not of coercion.

Another belief to which she strongly subscribes is the need for one's life to be God-centered rather than cause-centered. "The surrendered life might be a life surrendered to the church, to service, to missions, to temperance, to peace, to a certain interpretation of doctrines, and even to prayer, and still fall short of the will of God," she asserted. "The surrendered life must be to God as revealed in Jesus Christ our Lord. It is not a commitment to a cause, or to an institution. It is a commitment to a Person, the divine Person, first of all."

All of her life she has held profound personal convictions about many issues which faced the church. In the early years of her life some of the more controversial issues before the church included the wearing of the plain garb and the prayer veil, higher education, open communion and alliance with the temperance movement (a pertinent political issue in the twenties and thirties). Later issues related to the church's stance on pacifism, the role of women in contemporary society and the church, the many diverse problems relating to human sexuality and human rights and the ecological problems that developed in relation to use of the earth's natural resources. These and other issues were of genuine concern to Anna, yet she has never become strongly identified with one side or another on any specific issue. Why?

In discussing this with her several factors emerged. One is the attitude of militancy and extremism which are all too often the hallmarks of leaders in groups working toward the achievement of specific objectives. Extremism in any form bothers her, especially if it is the kind that tends to alienate persons rather than bring them together. On occasion those involved in achieving a specific objective become so zealous in their actions and statements that they turn persons against the church itself. "I feel that my role is to point them to my Lord and then let them struggle individually with what He would do in any given situation," she pointed out. "When we discuss *what* we believe, we are divided, but when we discuss *Whom* we believe, we come together." For her, His life, His way is the only answer and as she succinctly stated: "He drew men to His way by His forgiving love and by going to the cross for them, not by trying to force them to His stance by a moral edict." She concluded: "Doctrines are important, interpretations are important. But when the 'defenders of the faith' get on the warpath sometimes God seems to be forgotten."

This effort to avoid jumping on the bandwagon of specific causes was not always fully understood. For instance: a few individuals involved in the women's liberation movement, both within and without the church, found it difficult to understand why Anna did not embrace this cause with real ardor. There were those who felt strongly that she should take a public stand on some issues that to them were of great importance. Comments were not always gracious from some persons when she asserted her independence in this and other matters.

On the opposite side of the coin are those of Anna's own generation, both men and women, who feel that she is "too liberated." A few of these do not fully appreciate what they consider to be her "too liberal theology." Then, too, there probably are some who struggle with personal envy because of the fact that she has been so successful in a predominantly male world of teaching and preaching. This happened decades before the concept of women's liberation as an assertive social movement was even conceived. As one of her fellow teachers at Bethany pointed out in later years: "Before women's lib you were women's liberation . . . . You were accepted as an equal on the Bethany faculty and made your own unique contribution in Christian education and in the life of the Spirit."

There was at least one pastor who felt rewarded by her allegiance to the apostle Paul. He wrote a letter expressing appreciation for one of her books and her service to the church. Apparently discouraged by what he felt to be unwarranted attacks on his favorite apostle by some ardent feminists who did not fully understand the background of Paul's writing and preaching, he concluded his letter with: " . . . . and it does me good to read after a woman who has a genuine appreciation of the Apostle Paul!"

Anna is deeply sensitive to the needs and feelings of all persons with whom she has dealt. She, however, is never unduly upset by adverse criticism from those who differ with her either from a theological standpoint or in her lifestyle and choices. She is so secure in her own personhood that the criticism of her contemporaries, justified or unjustified, can also be accepted with a loving spirit. Sometimes criticism is actually welcomed. When an observation is made that is less than flattering, she often says: "I needed that for my growth!" Such security is all too rare in an insecure world. It comes from an inner self that finds its peace in a value system founded upon solid rock, a value system that takes into account those things that are permanent and changeless.

Anna believes in *fellowship*. For her there was a bit of God in every life that touched hers whether for moments, minutes or months. She received new insights from the cab driver, the hairdresser, the grocery clerk, the seatmate on a trip, those with whom she worked, taught, lived and worshiped. There is no such thing to Anna as an inconsequential human encounter.

A friend once described her as a "professional in fellowship." There has probably not been a more apt one-line portrait of Anna. Fellowship took place within the many homes where she lived with her family and in the hundreds of homes where she herself has been a guest. For Anna, good food, stimulating conversation and the warmth of hospitality are all overflowing evidence of God's love within the lives of persons. Real fellowship is not contrived, not formally planned and never carried out because of a sense of duty. It grows out of love for each other because one was first loved by God and then loved Him in return through other persons. It is the overflow.

There was spiritual fellowship, too. The Ashrams, countless meetings in churches, camps and colleges were times in which she could feed others spiritually as well as receive spiritual nourishment for her own soul. She realized, however, that even spiritual nourishment could be overdone if it was a means of running away from the humdrum realities of everyday living. Speaking of those who isolate themselves from the pain of the real world by trying to stay perpetually in a spiritually stimulating and protected environment, she commented' "If we are being sent into the world we can never remain huddled together in a fellowship caucus!" Anna believes in fellowship, but it is within the context of everyday life, not in a dream world of imagination and isolation.

She believes in a *disciplined* life. Hers is not the discipline of asceticism which demands discipline merely for the sake of discipline. Neither is it discipline for the sake of reaching an accomplished objective. Rather, it is a discipline born of love and desire to be in total obedience to the will of

God; discipline to a way of life which calls forth the best she can give in service to Him and to humankind. "Jesus' prayer life was not a religious discipline," according to Anna. "It was a discipline of love, with understanding of commitment to the will of his Father."

Very early in life she learned the discipline of love within the framework of obedience. On January 18, 1895, when she was not quite two years old, her father wrote in his diary: "I spanked Annie for the first time. Was done effectively. She's quiet tonight when told. How nice to have obedient children! I intend to train mine to obey, then they'll love me more." Father Beahm apparently had some reservations about spanking as a method of discipline, however. Two days later he wrote: "Annie's spanking is working charmingly. Proper whipping is a marvelously good investment. But once I thought it all a farce, and worse. We learn 'as the days go by'!"

One is led to wonder if Anna's obedience to her heavenly Father came about naturally because she had learned to respect and obey an earthly father who loved her dearly. She learned early there were restrictions within which one must live and that living within the restrictions because of love was much easier than doing so because of fear.

Although Anna has been an ardent student of the Bible and believes in the power of prayer, her concept of a disciplined devotional life is not a "chapter a day, so many minutes in prayer" kind of exercise. It is more like that of the cook in an ancient French monastery, Nicholas Herman, better known as Brother Lawrence. His was the "practice of the presence of God" kind of discipline. One sentence epitomized his life: "When the appointed times of prayer were passed, he found no difference, because he still continued with God, praising and blessing Him with all his might, so that he passed his life in continual joy." Brother Lawrence was not in conscious prayer all the time, but as he himself said he always tried to be responsive to God's "inward drawings."

This responsiveness, this surge of the soul Godward is the kind of spiritual discipline symbolic of Sister Anna. She is as much in prayer while baking one of her famous cherry pies for Baxter as she is on her knees in the holy of holies. "The time of business," wrote Brother Lawrence, "does not differ from the time of prayer, and in the noise and clatter of my kitchen, while several persons are at the same time calling for different things, I possess God in as great tranquility as if I were upon my knees at the Blessed Sacrament." The serenity of Sister Anna during times of strain and stress was due in no small part to this same kind of spiritual discipline.

The solid foundation for all her credo is an unquenchable belief in the Fatherhood of God, in the Personhood of Jesus the Christ and in the Holy Spirit as the agent and mediator of Christ's living Presence in the world. Anna never felt the need to prove or argue the fine theological points of the triune Godhead or of any other theological tenets or dogmas which tend to divide the Christian faith into so many fragmented segments.

In her preaching, she has often referred to the fact that it will be a great day when we will not have to explain or defend the faith, only proclaim and live it. For her, learning to live by the code of love as exemplified in the life of the Christ is the only answer to the human search for meaning in life. It is the only and final answer to the preservation of the human species on the increasingly crowded spaceship earth. Her firm faith in the ultimate triumph of good over evil is so secure that the issue needs little discussion, no defense. In her theology, love cannot be killed, God cannot be destroyed. It is the solid rock on which her life's credo is built.

What are some of her methods, her rules for living based on her beliefs? To attempt a description of Anna's method is a little like trying to paint a word picture of a butterfly in flight. One simply has to see it to believe it. Anetta C. Mow, her sister-in-law, was a student with her at Bethany. They also served on the India mission field at the same time and lived near each other in Chicago while Anna taught at Bethany and Anetta C. worked on the staff of the Church of the Brethren in Elgin, Illinois. A letter written by Anetta C. at the time of Anna's retirement from the seminary described in a cryptic fashion some of Anna's "methodology."

> She learned to do forty things at once. Saw the pyramids, studied Gujarati. Superb cook, Southern biscuits, uncounted rice and curry dinners. Held "Open House" often. Taught Chinese Sunday school. Cared for her invalid mother. Graded stacks of papers. Dashed off dozens of letters. Taught in summer camps and youth conferences . . . Enjoyed shopping, painting dragons on her stairway. Cut and sewed up bolts of cloth, including coats for her friends. Answered 100,001 telephone calls. Felt equally at ease with the rich and the poor. Kept the home filled with things educational and inspirational. Loved the grandchildren. Wrote articles for the church papers. Served three terms as member of the General Board . . . The marvel is not that she left a few things undone but that she did so much . . .

Another writer, Inez Long, in describing Anna's method for getting things done wrote:

> Simultaneously, she catches ideas for a speech spread out on the desk, turns the pages of a current book she is reading, finishes off with a dash of Oriental seasoning the meal of curry and rice cooking on the stove while all the time she is entertaining guests in a crowded apartment. Her system of getting things done has no obvious order. Yet she handles many items from a hidden efficiency of her own so that each turns out as planned.

This hidden efficiency is based on several things. Hers is a life centered in others, not self-centered, and concerned with giving and not getting. Her life is centered on *people*, not *things*. Housekeeping is kept as simple as possible. In Anna's book of values it is much more important to "keep the house" than to allow the house to keep her. Making a warm and loving home atmosphere is always more important than spotless housekeeping. This is an attribute remembered by her adult children as one of special importance. A grateful son wrote:

There was an almost unlimited and self-sacrificing caring for her family. She kept me alive when I had very serious malaria by staying up all night with an ice pack. She would go all out in dinners for us when we were home from college or school. She cared for my wife when we had our third child. Always there was acceptance and understanding . . . As a mother, she always believed in encouraging her children to make up their own minds, and she allowed us a kind of responsibility which is rare. I was in China when still 20, under somewhat dangerous circumstances. No doubt she worried, but she had the discipline to be confident in us and to allow life to take its course—with faith.

One of Anna's missionary colleagues told of being in her home for a meeting when the Mow children were young. While she was there, the children's pet guinea pig was conducting some important business of her own—producing a new litter of babies. The obstetric ward was a box behind the stove in the room where their meeting took place. At frequent intervals the children came in to check on the mother's progress and squealed with delight as they announced the arrival of each new baby. According to her recollection this frank, uninhibited birthing process was shocking to a few of the more traditionally minded persons present. For her, it was a demonstration of Anna's innate wisdom in allowing the children the opportunity to learn the basic realities of life. It was another evidence of her methodology: acceptance of life with complete openness, utter candor.

This episode demonstrates two more of Anna's gifts: her *ability to adapt to circumstances* and her *spontaneity*. She has been described by one who knows her well as "utterly unflappable." The art of taking the ups and downs of life in stride, of adjusting to change when change was called for has stood her in good stead throughout her long and busy career. Many different homes, different responsibilities, different challenges in terms of her life's work were adjusted to with grace. No doubt her extraordinary energy and vitality are partly due to the fact that no energy was wasted in regret or indecision. Decision-making is done thoughtfully and prayerfully, but when it is done, it is done. Her priorities demand that distractions are dealt with rapidly and finally.

Hers is a life *tuned to the timelessness of God*. She lives fully each and every moment yet she knows that the long range consequences are what really matter. She has learned patience. She is able to plant a seed of thought with a person and then wait for its development. She does not attempt to take over the work of the Holy Spirit or of God. "The main energy crisis in the world is not a lack of oil," she once said. "It is that we're trying to do God's work in our own strength." She pointed out that we are too eager for things to happen according to our own timetables and not God's. To illustrate the human propensity for hurrying things up she often tells the story of one of her children who planted some seeds and then pulled the plants out of the ground every few days after they had sprouted to see if they were growing. At the heart of Anna's methodology is the art of giving God time to do His part in the resolution of human problems.

One of her most frequently stated maxims is: "You have to begin with people where they are." There is little doubt that this understanding is one of her most effective tools for helping persons who are in a state of spiritual, mental or emotional confusion. The complete acceptance of persons at their own level of understanding plus her obvious love and concern for them has made her a peerless counselor and confidante. Her sympathetic ear is also a most discerning one. She even listens with her heart to those persons who do not have anything to say aloud.

This technique was discovered by a co-leader who worked with Anna in a small group which was meeting daily over a period of time for the purpose of study, sharing and spiritual growth. The co-leader adamantly insisted that everyone had to participate, everyone had to say something. It happened that prior to the first meeting of the group the husband of one of the members confided to Anna that his wife just would not talk. According to him she never had anything to say at home or anywhere else.

Knowing this, Anna was aware of "where she was, where she was coming from."

Too much pressure was put on this quiet woman by Anna's leader-colleague who was obsessed by her newly learned techniques of group dynamics. Consequently the woman simply withdrew further into her protective shell of silence. Meantime, Anna had been singling her out for attention privately. She was praying for her daily, asking her about her children, asking her opinion on certain things, getting to know her as a person and most of all just showing her that she cared.

On the final day of the small group sessions, after a few leading questions by Anna, the woman opened up and made some very good observations much to the surprise of everyone present. At a later time when the two leaders were evaluating their work, the other leader remarked to Anna: "I've been watching you all week. You did everything wrong that could possibly have been done according to the rules, yet you were able to get this woman to talk and I wasn't. How did you do it?" For Anna, the answer was obvious: she began with her where she was. Furthermore, she *cared*. These two things served to penetrate the shell of loneliness within which the woman had lived and suffered.

Another important facet of Anna's methodology is a dedication to the concept of *continuing growth*. Nels Ferré, a fellow theologian as well as a dear friend, taught her that "real faith never lets itself become embalmed." The need for growth, for the continuing search for new truth, is immensely important to Anna. Her dedication to the discernment of God's direction for her life is never outgrown. She has no illusions that growing into the likeness of Christ is easy. Learning to "speak the truth in love," learning that forgiveness is a continuing process, learning that she must be humble enough to *be taught* as well as to teach, learning the fine arts of patience, of hoping when all appears hopeless and of having faith when there seems to be little reason for faith—all these are lessons in living that were not mastered in one fell swoop. It is a lifetime process of becoming.

Anna's commitment to the concept of growth keeps her

open to the discovery of new truth, the discovery of "what differences *do* matter and what differences don't," as she expressed it. She learned early in life that one needed to distinguish between what was tradition and what was truth.

When only fifteen years old, Anna went with her father to Philadelphia for a communion service at the Germantown church. All of the services she had attended prior to that time had taken place in rural congregations where there had been much emphasis placed on the traditional way of conducting communion. Most of the women in attendance at these meetings wore the "plain garb" which was the mode of the day for most members of the church. All of the women wore prayer veils at communion. Beef sandwiches, communion soup and communion bread were all prepared according to traditional methods. These were important elements of the "love feast" and the total communion service.

What a surprise at Philadelphia! The women were dressed in the contemporary styles of the day. Many of them did not have prayer veils on their heads. Cheese and crackers were served at the love feast instead of beef and soup. But the most amazing thing of all for young Anna was the fact that her father made no comment whatsoever about the strange way the Philadelphians observed the sacred service. This experience taught her that there is more than one way for things to be done, even things as serious as the communion service. It was the *spirit* of what was happening that really mattered. One must not get all hung up on the traditions which sometimes tend to confuse rather than clarify the truth.

One final story about Anna's unorthodox methodology that really worked was shared by a young minister who worked with her in a spiritual life retreat for a large group of youth. He was inexperienced in group leadership but he had studied some current literature about group dynamics and the various sure-fire techniques for drawing out the feelings and ideas of youth. There were a lot of "be sures" according to him. Be sure to get everyone in a good mood before beginning; crack some jokes, get them involved with light conversation. Be sure everyone is on the same level; don't stand or sit on a level higher than your group. Be sure they're seated informally; put them in semicircles—straight rows are a disaster for group interchange—and by all means seat them on the floor if possible. Be sure you don't talk about your own experiences; that's too egotistical, it'll turn them off for sure. Be sure you don't act as an obvious leader; that is too threatening to those you are leading. Be sure you don't get too serious, too "preachy." There were a few more "be sures"—but this is *his* story and here's the way he told it.

> We met first as a total group. Sister Anna made her presentation and then I made mine. We divided into two groups. My group was sent to the basement, hers was to remain in the sanctuary. This suited me fine because in the basement we could sit on the floor. I could be on their level. We could be in semicircles, no straight, stiff rows.
>
> I started off with some jokes, some singing to put them at ease. From then on, everything went downhill, but fast! Everybody just sat. They didn't appear to be very interested in anything. They didn't have any questions about either of our speeches. It was like pulling eye teeth to get most of them to say anything at all. Of course there were the usual few who wanted to talk all the time—especially if they had a chance to say something funny or be cute. We were supposed to have one hour for discussion. Finally at the end of forty-five miserable, unproductive minutes I simply gave up. I dismissed my group with the feeble excuse that they might want a short break before the next session.
>
> On my way upstairs I heard the group in the sanctuary laughing loudly. I decided to step in the back and see what, if anything, Sister Anna had going. Well! There was plenty. Those kids were holding their hands up and waving them in the air, wanting to ask questions. Everybody seemed to want to get into the act. They were all *interested* in everything that was being said. And Sister Anna was doing everything wrong. At least it seemed so according to the book.
>
> The kids were all seated in straight, stiff rows on uncomfortable church pews. She was telling them

stories about herself, about her own experiences, of all things! She was waving her arms and making pointed gestures just like she was *preaching*! And all of those young people were just eating it up. They were talking about really dry, serious things: the demands God makes on those who expect to be His disciples; what it means to love with agape love instead of the Hollywood kind; how one goes about becoming reconciled to another . . . They finished out their hour and didn't want to quit. They went for fifteen minutes more. They still weren't ready. Finally at about 20 minutes past the time they stopped their discussion and rolled out of there like they had been on a high — a spiritual high, that is.

I learned some things that weekend about what it takes to get youth going. It had to do with something far more important than rules and regulations, with superficial techniques memorized from a book. It had to do with the *Spirit of a Person* within a *person*, Sister Anna. It works. Those kids recognized and responded to the real thing when they saw it.

Anna would not have wanted the young leader to remain crestfallen. Her years of experience had taught her that the hunger in the hearts of human beings was the same in every generation: the hunger to be loved, to be accepted, to find meaning in life. She talked about these needs with the youth of three generations from her own rich life experiences, and to this they always responded. The meaning of life for her was to know and love God. Sharing this was no dreary duty but a joyous, energizing experience. It was something to which youth would always respond, in any culture, in any generation.

If Christ's glory was the only real reason for being, then why should she not follow his methodology? His simple stories, his penetrating, never-ending questions? His ever-drawing, self-sacrificing love? If it worked for Him, why not for her? It was toward the goal of a deeper relationship with Him that she challenged youth again and again. And, in the words of the surprised young seminarian: "It worked!"

Chapter 7

Mother . . . and More

Relationship is a key word with Sister Anna. Relationship to God, to family, to all one's fellow human beings. She seems to have an instinctive recognition of the fact that one cannot be fully human, really fulfilled, without relationship. What happens between persons is more important than rites and rituals and a warm and loving relationship with people is the central focus of her religious witness to the world.

She often makes succinct observations to point up her belief in the importance of one's interaction with another. "Your spiritual growth is advanced or hindered by your success or failure in human relationships," she has asserted emphatically on numerous occasions. One of the questions she raised in her writing and speaking was that of one's relationships within the family circle. "Have you ever realized that your relationship to your mate is the test of your relationship with God?" This thought-provoking question no doubt caused some serious pondering on the part of many of her readers and hearers.

First and foremost is one's relationship to God. For Sister Anna, having God at the center of one's being provides the cohesive force which holds all human relationships intact. Believing there was a bit of God in every person she met, Anna felt the more people she could love the more real God would become in her own life as well as in the lives of those she touched. God's love is like a fountain: it shoots forth and then receives back into its source the drops of water that fly into the air while reflecting the sunlight like millions of diamonds. For Anna, those bits of God's Spirit, flowing and ebbing between persons, mean relationship. This is one's reason for being.

Next to God, her love of family is the central fountain from which she draws her strength. One of her basic tenets for good family relationships was setting the members free to be themselves. She appreciated this from her husband Baxter. She gave the same gift to her children. After nurturing them physically, emotionally and spiritually to adulthood she turned them loose. Anna once said, "I suppose the hardest thing I ever had to say to my daughter was what was said just before she got married: 'Lois, we love you dearly but from here on you belong to Ernie more than you do to us.'" All strings to her children were untied when they went out into the world on their own. "But our love for them increased with the passing years," she stated. In her later years her children have provided much spiritual and emotional support for her. "Sometimes when I'm discouraged and low spiritually," she said in her 89th year, "I just call up Merrill and talk a while with him and soon he has me feeling encouraged and believing that everything is going to be all right." In a time of hospitalization, her daughter Lois came to be with her and the warmth between them made bystanders believe Anna felt the operation was worthwhile just to have Lois with her for several days!

In 1973, Anna's youngest sister, Lois B. Eyles, and the members of her church, First Church of the Brethren in Roanoke, Virginia, placed Anna's name in nomination for the *Mother of the Year Award* for the State of Virginia. Her pastor, the Reverend Paul Alwine, was asked to prepare a statement about her life, to be used in support of the nomination. He wrote:

> How do you describe the beauty of a sunset so that a reader can see it? How do you tell of the gentle breezes so that the reader feels it? How do you relate the warmth of human understanding so that the reader will be touched by it? These are the questions facing anyone who attempts to write about Sister Anna and her religious experience. It is beautiful, it is gentle, it is warm . . . Now what does all of this say about Sister Anna as a mother? It says that her children had the extreme good fortune of having a mother who loved them but did not smother them, who had ideas about

life but did not impose them, who could appreciate their individuality and let them develop their own lifestyle . . . While her three children are deeply religious they are not carbon copies . . . The continuing bond of affection which Sister Anna has for her family and they for her speaks dramatically of a religious experience where the love of God and the kind of freedom it offers is the key. Her religion is not words, printed or spoken. Her religion is an authentic lifestyle that attracts young and old alike. It would be an honor to Virginia to have her chosen as Mother of the Year.

And she was! The attending festivities were long to be remembered by all who had the good fortune to participate.

On March 7, 1973, surrounded by about forty of her relatives and closest friends along with several former Virginia Mothers, Anna was presented this framed citation by Governor Lynwood Holton:

> Devoted mother who has strengthened the moral and spiritual foundations of her home throughout the years . . .
> Who has reared her children in reverence for God in an atmosphere of love, sympathy and understanding . . .
> Whose successful public service to her community and state has been widely recognized . . .
> Who through prayer in her home and by public example has contributed to the religious life about her and advanced the ecumenical concept of Brotherhood and International Good Will . . .
>
> ANNA BEAHM MOW

beloved by all who know her, is hereby honored by the American Mothers' Committee, Inc. as the Mother of Virginia, 1973.

> Signed: Mrs. R. G. LeTourneau
> President
> American Mothers' Committee, Inc.

In a long letter describing the occasion to their two

sons and other close relatives, Baxter wrote: "The Governor shook hands with everyone. Being a Roanoker himself, Mr. Holton was especially happy to welcome the Roanoke delegation. And Anna professed that she was not sure whether these had come to see her or to meet him!" Her typical quip and the hearty laughter that followed provided precisely the right touch to the dignified occasion.

The state honor was happily and graciously received but the citation which pleased Anna most and the one she showed to friends who came to call was the special plaque prepared for her by the eldest three of her granddaughters. It was hand lettered in beautiful Old English script and declared:

> In the twenty-five years of dedicated service,
>
> GRANDMOTHER OF THE YEAR, 1973
>
> by the authority invested in us.
>
> Barbara, Kathy, Loanne

Following the formalities in the Governor's office there was a luncheon in Richmond's famous old John Marshall Hotel, and it was a pleasurable climax to the well-deserved honor.

In May, Anna went to Denver, Colorado, for the four days of festivities surrounding the selection of the American Mother of the Year. She was accompanied by her daughter, Lois Snavely, and her youngest sister, Lois B. Eyles. There she was in competition with fifty-one State Mothers for the national honor. As part of the contest each of the mothers stood beneath a flower-bedecked arbor to make a brief statement about herself as well as her family. The closing of Anna's short speech reflected her own philosophical and spiritual bent toward childrearing:

> We thank God for his love and guidance through the years; we know that His word never fails. I pray that I may always be true to the words expressed by Tagore, the great Indian poet, as he spoke for a mother: "Let my love, like sunlight, surround you and

give you illumined freedom."

"She looked lovely," wrote a proud daughter Lois to the other family members. "She wore the gray and gold sari that Mrs. Pandit gave her and the orchid corsage we put in her hair made her look like the queen she was."

In describing the awards banquet Lois wrote: "As soon as the blessing was said by a Jewish rabbi the announcement of the National Mother of the Year was made . . . Mrs. Ruth Youngblood from Minnesota. She is the one that mother wanted to win, but Mrs. Glave (a former Virginia Mother) was frankly disappointed. She felt that mother had the more credentials and should have gotten it."

Immediately following the four days in Denver, Anna flew off to Ohio for a meeting. This "mother business," as she facetiously called all the excitement surrounding her honor, was now over and she had to get back to her life's true love: God's business.

Anna's family relationships extend far beyond blood relatives. In addition to her children, grandchildren, sisters and brother, plus dozens of cousins, uncles and aunts, there was her adopted family. There was Pervin Christian, a lovely Parsee girl in India who had been disowned and disinherited by her family when she became a Christian. To her the Mows were true parents. They not only provided her with moral and spiritual support but also with substantial financial support. She was left a widow with no means to care for herself and her partially blind child. For years the Mows sent checks regularly to help provide for their needs. Pervin wrote many letters to her "Precious Mother." This paragraph shows her deep dependence and need for the kind of help they gave her: "I am a woman of stout heart and have stood endless sufferings, yet have maintained my high and jovial spirit, but now at this stage I find myself — I do not know what to say!! Dear Mother, a letter from you becomes a stream in the desert! A spark in the darkness!"

There was also Beatriz deMeyehlis Kloch. She became the Mows' daughter after she came to America. Her own mother had died in Goa and she had come to the states to complete her education. After receiving her doctor of philosophy degree from Loyola University in Chicago she became a counselor at Hines Military Hospital.

There was Henry Solanky, a young Indian boy whom the Mows helped to educate in order that he might work more effectively among the Christians they left behind in India. There was also Gersham Jivanji, a young Indian Christian who became a minister and who always considered Anna his "spiritual mother." Gersham died several years ago but the Mows still keep in touch with his widow and contribute to her financial support.

There was Ben Wati, a young Indian student who considered the Mow home his home during the years he was in Chicago attending college. After his return to India to live and work among his own village people, Anna was instrumental in setting up an appointment for him with Prime Minister Nehru to discuss the problems of his people. (This contact was made possible because of Anna's long and enduring friendship with Madame Pandit, Nehru's sister.) After his official visit, a grateful Mr. Wati wrote Anna:

> When the time was up he indicated that I could write to him. This I did the same day . . . He replied to my letter, just the day before he left for the USA. That showed the value he placed on our talks and the importance of the problem, at least within India . . . Though nothing spectacular will come of my talk, I at least feel richly rewarded for this personal contact. It was entirely on a friendly basis—and all because of *you*.

There was Vartkes Ketenjian, another young man who received help, both spiritual and financial, while in school in Chicago. The list could go on and on, an entire host of "love children" were included in Anna's extended family. There were dozens of seminary students, both men and women, for whom she filled the role of spiritual mother. Harold Bomberger, one of these students, wrote on the occasion of her selection as Virginia's Mother of the Year:

> This is a tremendous honor and Betty and I would like to share in wishing you well. There is a sense in

which you have been the mother to a number of generations of pastors, laymen and churchmen in the Church of the Brethren. Then, too, because of your involvement with E. Stanley Jones and many other Christian groups, you have extended your motherhood worldwide.

This short note no doubt pleased her as much as the accolade from her fellow Roanoker, Governor Linwood Holton.

There is one area of Anna's overflowing fountain-of-love relationship that few persons know about unless they themselves are in pain. It is her letter writing and counseling ministry. Over a period of years, hundreds of persons have written to her about every conceivable human problem. Marital infidelity, divorce, wife and child abuse, mental illness and mental retardation, homosexuality, alcoholism, spiritual dryness—there is not a human problem that she has not given help with at one time or another.

Those asking for help come from every walk of life. There are letters written on lined tablet paper, sometimes 10-15 pages in length from persons, both men and women, pouring out their pain. There are letters typed on business or professional letterheads, obviously from persons holding responsible positions. One wrote seeking her advice "because you have more common sense about this matter than anyone I know." There are letters from aging friends pouring out their pain and frustration because they saw directions taken by their churches which frightened and disturbed them. Letters from youth indicate frustration for other reasons.

There were letters on expensive monogrammed stationery from the wife of a professional man who had lived for years with the knowledge of her husband's infidelity. As she returned home from a trip he met her with the gift of a shining new Cadillac. "Anna, I wanted to be elated," she wrote. "Most women would jump for joy, and I couldn't find any feeling whatever . . . Frankly, I am embarrassed to drive down the street . . . I really think he wants to appear kind and generous, which he is, if I can overlook his affairs.

The Cadillac is not because he wants to show me his love. He wants to show the town how *good* he is to me. The car is perfect bait for getting his ego stroked."

Some write of terrible frustration because they appear "outwardly successful" but they are "inwardly miserable." One woman wrote in lonely exasperation: "I know what makes for tranquility, I just have the devil of a time practicing it. I want somebody besides God to meet me halfway! When that never happens I feel so hopeless." Hers was an echo of many letters, many aching hearts. They knew Anna would understand—and she did. Many times she has been able to help those who write to better understand their own contribution to a problem situation.

Letters involving divorce and child-custody proceedings are common. Several have echoed the heartbreak of the woman who wrote: "I would like you to know that I am a Christian. For the past year I have been contemplating divorce. Even the mention of this word makes me shudder, but the situation in my home is becoming unbearable and I can't believe that a God of love wants a child of His to endure in an impossible situation." On the outside of each envelope Anna writes the date each letter is received and answered. At the end of one letter, in her large scrawling handwriting was this notation: "P.S. 1982. A close friend now. Family together . . . " The original plea for help had been written eleven years before. She had kept in touch with them intermittently all that time!

Many of those who confide in her are ministers and/or their wives or family members. Because of the nature of their own professional standing in a community some found it difficult to seek professional help and so they turned to her. One ended his sad and agonizing eight-page letter with: "I'm so scared. Please continue your prayers for us. No need to write, just pray." A woman friend wrote in behalf of a friend of hers who was contemplating remarriage after being divorced: "Anna, this scenario no doubt has been repeated to you many times as it seems so many people are seeking divorce these days. I am sure many discuss it with you."

How much time Anna spends in writing to, praying for

and counseling with persons will never be known. Much of the counseling has taken place by long-distance telephone calls. From all over the country persons "reach out to touch" this warm and responsive person with whom they feel safe in baring their deepest feelings and emotions. She not only provides them with spiritual succor but with good, common-sense advice.

Her loving acceptance of the "sinner if not the sin," her broad knowledge of human behavior, her realistic view of existence, and above all, her deep understanding of the role God can play in a person's life have made her a counselor beyond compare. She has never preached to those in pain, never probed deeper than they were ready to go and she never stands in judgment of actions. Her love and concern communicate in such a way that she often has persons examining their own behavior in light of the love admonition of St. Paul. One of her favorite methods in both speaking and counseling is to challenge the hearer to read the 13th chapter of 1st Corinthians every day for six weeks, substituting the word "I" for the word "love" in every verse. Examining behavior in this fashion, many persons have been helped to recognize their own contribution to a problem situation. When this happened they were at least able to resolve half the problem. Frequently the reflective qualities of love worked their magic and if things weren't entirely healed they were at least helped.

Although Anna is a tender and truly loving person she can be firm when she feels it necessary. Those persons who make a career of sharing their personal problems with anyone and everyone who would listen have not always gained her sympathy. She has an innate understanding of human behavior that enables her to distinguish between those who truly need her help and those who merely want a "dumping bucket" for their own everyday frustrations.

Self-pity and self-centeredness are vigorously opposed by her and she can be somewhat ascerbic in her advice to those she feels are freely indulging in either. More than once she advised persons to "get off the judgment seat and climb up on the cross where you belong." "Self-centeredness is *child-stuff*," she once wrote. "It is not maturity and it is the fruit of resentment and self-pity." God at the center instead of self was the final answer to self-dethronement.

There are special persons from whom she received her own spiritual sustenance, those who are her spiritual brothers and sisters because they are a part of the family of God. These included her professional co-workers from the missionary and seminary days, the hundreds of students whom she taught and the thousands to whom she spoke at the Ashrams and other occasions. Once she participates deeply in the lives of persons she keeps in touch. Friends in depth are never discarded. The list is only added to by new places, new experiences.

A few have become very special to her because of deeply shared spiritual experiences that have taken place at various times. E. Stanley Jones, Nels Ferré, Eugenia Price, Rosa Page Welch, Madame Pandit—these are only a few of the very special ones who have at times ministered to her that she might minister to others. From them she learned and gained strength. For them she prayed and gave strength. This mutual caring has been an endless ebb and flow of God's Spirit in the deep tides of love that have been so evident in Anna's life.

Chapter 8
Speaking the Truth in Love

Anna's interest in human relationship is a definite factor in her lengthy career as an able spokesperson for God. Whether she speaks to 3,300 or 3,000 there is that intimate "I care about you" kind of informality in her speaking that makes her hearers feel she is speaking directly to their own specific need.

It has been said there are several tests by which to measure the success or failure of a public speaker's career. One, are persons in their audience interested? Two, are they in demand without that demand having to be created by a public relations bureau or other "behind the scenes" activity? Three — and probably the most acid test of all — do they get invited back? If these criteria are reliable measurements, then one can assert unequivocally that Anna is a premiere public speaker.

From the time she left India in 1940 until the publication of this biography, a span of 43 years, she had more requests for speaking engagements than she was able to fill. In the latter two decades she was usually booked at least two to three years in advance. There was no faithful secretary to answer all the letters of requests, no one to keep the dates organized and details for travel worked out, no one to pack her bags or be sure she "had everything." All of these bothersome details, handled for most public speakers by secretaries or wives, were arranged by Anna herself. In between she attended to all the many family responsibilities for which wives, mothers and grandmothers are held accountable.

A competent travel agency arranged ticketing. Two bags were kept partially packed at all times: a small one for short trips of two to four days and a larger one for trips extending from a week to two weeks. If plans had to be rearranged, it was she who attended to the details.

The idea of a public relations agent to secure speaking engagements for her would be a joke to Anna. Her agents are the hundreds of persons whose lives she has touched at one time or another. They know she has something important to share. They tell each other, they tell their friends. One might even venture to say that her most effective agent is that "Something" which creates a desire within many persons to hear the good news she has to share. Whatever it is, they come—again and again.

And they listen. People listen to what she has to say with genuine interest. An elderly admirer, capitalizing key words, wrote to Anna after hearing her speak for the first time:

> You are a very interesting Speaker and a Speaker that should be praised for the Great amount of Humor you get into your message. I am sure it keeps many people just a little Bit more AWAKE. I have seen people in church when some ministers were speaking shut their eyes. But I did not see anyone shut their eyes when you were speaking . . . I feel sure that when Christ spoke when he was here on earth no one sat around with their eyes closed.

That radiant, vibrant spirit of Anna's simply shakes people out of the spiritual lethargy which sometimes prompts the "closed" eye.

As for being invited back a second time, if this *is* the acid test for a speaker, Anna's record is exceptional. She was invited for return engagements over and over again. At times it seemed as if those who were hungering and thirsting after the Word could scarcely get enough of it if it was delivered by Sister Anna.

Several personal attributes help to contribute to her effectiveness as a speaker. Her marvelous sense of humor is surely one of her most potent assets. Yet her keen ability to balance this with very serious truths is legendary. Her sense of timing, knowing when to inject humor and when not to, is remarkable. Her delivery is an informal, person-to-person style that makes everyone present feel she is speaking directly to them. In a clear, crisp, concise style she drives home her serious points, sometimes making her listeners squirm but never leaving them truly injured. She does not turn her audience off with language that is too preachy or too complex to comprehend.

Anna uses personal experiences copiously yet she is seldom accused of being egotistical or of promoting her own interests. Her stories are told to illustrate a pertinent point and are seldom flat and tedious. Rarely do Anna's speeches sound canned. Long years of experience have taught her the value of having tailor-made speeches, geared or slanted to a specific audience. She knows how to take the emotional temperature of her audience and speak to their need accordingly. Her speeches are usually brief, concise and to the point. She knows when to quit. Once when addressing an audience of about seven hundred persons, she made her final statement, said a hearty "Amen" and was well on her way toward her seat before the astonished listeners could believe it was all over. She mastered well the theatrical art of quitting while she was ahead.

Thorough preparation has given her confidence in speaking. Knowing her Lord gives her authority. Her long years of study and teaching and her very obvious love for and joy in her Master makes it easy for listeners to trust in the truth she brings to them. She *believes* in what she shares. It isn't *her* word, it is God's—she is merely the instrument through which it is transmitted. But she is no apologetic, halfhearted medium. She has something to say that could affect one's life for now and for eternity and she knows it. The truths she has imparted through the years are not shallow ones; they have substance; they make demands. Hers is an all-or-nothing kind of faith in which she believes implicitly.

Anna's greatest gift as a speaker, however, has been her love for those to whom she speaks. She cares about the personal problems with which they struggle. She cares about the doubts aroused in their minds by inept and inaccurate interpretations of the Bible by those who sometimes twisted the truths of God's word to serve their own prejudicial purposes. She cares about the pain caused for the spiritually sensitive by the spiritually insensitive. Sister Anna *cares*.

She began caring early, teaching Sunday school classes while in her teens. Opportunities for speaking came in India where she was discovered to have a very special gift for working with children and youth. During her years at Bethany she had more opportunities and invitations to speak than she could fill due to her teaching and family responsibilities. She was frequently a guest speaker in the churches of many denominations in the greater Chicago area. It was also during this period that she began working in a special way with the youth of the nation.

Under the joint sponsorship of the Federal Council of Churches of Christ in America and the United Student Christian Council she began to participate in Religious Emphasis Week activities in a number of universities and colleges in the Midwest. The purpose of these weeks was to present the challenge of the Christian message to youth on campuses as a means of solving the ills of the world. This excerpt from a speech at Southern Illinois University, in November 1947, gives one an idea of the kind of challenge she presented to four decades of students.

> The real problem is in the hearts and minds of men. It is not a problem of physics but of ethics. It is easier to denature plutonium (another fission agent discovered since uranium) than to denature the evil spirit of man. What frightens us is not the explosive power of the atom bomb, but the equally explosive power of the human personality. Man's skills have outstripped his morals. His engineering has leaped ahead of his wisdom. He cannot cancel or call back his scientific advancement, but we can, we MUST, if the world is to survive, help man to catch up. In God's name, if you still believe in God, take Him seriously, and somehow get control of what science has given the world, or else—or else we shall all likewise perish.

That timely message of almost forty years ago is being

revived on college and university campuses today with a new urgency in the face of the nuclear possibilities. And Anna is still addressing the issues with her same challenge: to make life God-centered rather than self-centered. She is received with the same enthusiasm the students of a generation ago gave her. The acting Dean of an eastern college wrote her in April, 1977:

> In the three years that I have been associated with this college I have not heard students ask as many questions during the kind of seminar that we had as students asked of you the night that you shared with us. Generally, students when they are asked to question just sit there and look rather than ask for clarification or share whatever is upon their minds. I think by virtue of the fact that they were asking questions means that they were responding to what you shared with us.

In addition to her meetings on college and university campuses and her sermons in churches, she spoke to many civic organizations and other groups. Salvation Army personnel, Red Cross volunteers, spiritual life institutes and retreats for local churches, women's clubs, senior citizens, Women Aglow Fellowships—all of these and many others were participants in Anna's spiritual feasts. Evidence that she was appreciated as a speaker before all of these diverse groups was demonstrated by the warm letters of appreciation received from so many who were responsible for inviting her.

The executive director of a large city YMCA wrote: "Your genuineness of spirit, your effective presentation and your knowledge combined to make you one of the most discussed and appreciated of all our leaders for the week." A Massachusetts minister wrote in his church newsletter after a weekend retreat with her his appreciation for " . . . the simplicity with which she dispelled the wordiness and fogginess of dogma and doctrine, and the keenness of her wit." A grateful woman listener wrote:

> The reality of your message, the candidness and

tact with which you present your views, the beauty of your ability to disagree with someone at the same time taking nothing from the person with whom you disagree, the great knowledge and varied experiences you willingly share, and the beauty of your own personhood; for all of these, my heartfelt thanks.

After Anna spent a weekend in his church, a pastor wrote: "You reminded us again of the central realities of our faith, the rock upon which we build . . . On Sunday your words contained many morsels which we'll be savoring for some time." His letter concerning the "many morsels" demonstrated a phenomenon which is almost a hallmark of Anna's public speaking: the short, pithy quotations of hers which are repeated again and again long after she has left the podium. Almost every sermon contains at least a half-dozen "one-liners" which are apt to be repeated by ministers in their sermons as well as by their parishioners. Those speakers who have enough of a following to be quoted are sometimes misquoted, too, but Anna chuckles good-naturedly when this happens.

It is interesting to note that Anna's preaching ministry began many years before her formal ordination took place. She began her ministry as such with missionary work in India but it was not until September 18, 1960, almost forty years later, that she was ordained into the full ministry. This took place in First Church of the Brethren, Roanoke, Virginia, the church to which she and Baxter moved their letters of membership after her retirement from Bethany Seminary. Her ordination sermon, entitled "Some to Be Prophets," was preached by Edward K. Zeigler, a former colleague on the India mission field during the decade of the thirties.

Her first preaching mission came shortly after she was ordained and subsequent years saw her conducting at least eight or ten such meetings each year. She also conducted a number of weekend institutes and retreats in local congregations or districts. Some congregations asked her to return year after year that they might learn new truth from her, gain new courage for living and be challenged to deeper levels of spiritual probing. This joyously gentle woman spoke in a down-to-earth, practical way of what it means to learn to love. And as she stated more than once: "As you grow in the meaning of love you will find that you have also discovered the real meaning of life which has eluded so many people." One of her pastor friends wrote: "Her ministry is not one of pious judgment or fear; it is one of love." That is Sister Anna's real secret of success.

There was no arena in which her gifts as a speaker and a spiritual leader were so fully utilized and appreciated as in the United Christian Ashram movement. This movement was initiated by Dr. E. Stanley Jones, a Christian missionary, and three other persons at Sat Tal, India, in 1930, ten years before Jones' return to the United States.

The word *Ashram* (pronounced Ah'shrum) is from the Indian Sanskrit, meaning a retreat, a place where a leader goes aside with his disciples and in a disciplined, corporate quest, they search for a deeper spiritual relationship with God. The American Christian Ashrams were begun in 1940 by Jones upon his return to the U.S. He was assisted in the early years of the movement by Jesse M. Bader, executive secretary of the Federal Council of Churches of Christ in America.

Ashram participants live together for a period of time, usually five to ten days, in an informal setting. They study, work, pray and play together with one motivating drive: that their Leader, Jesus the Christ, might become more dominant within their own personal lives. According to Dr. Jones' interpretation: "The Christian Ashram is a fellowship centered around Jesus Christ. The purpose of the fellowship is transformation. This is one of God's movements whereby discouraged, downhearted, or defeated people are transformed into joyous, vigorous and victorious Christians through the transforming grace of Christ. We do not simply talk about the Kingdom of God, we become the Kingdom. People come as they are and are transformed into what God wants them to be." Their goal is to become God-centered individuals, not only for the period while they are in the Ashram, but also for the time when they must return to the routine of daily living.

Manmade barriers have no place in the Christian Ashram. There are no denominational barriers; persons from every faith and creed participate. Theological and denominational differences are set aside as participants search for the "mind of Christ" on personal matters as well as in their corporate worship and decision-making. Confession of spiritual needs is a central part of the Ashram fellowship. Said one Ashram participant: "Here we find the grace to remove our facades, come out from behind our pretenses and actually share our real needs."

Participants in the movement come from all walks of life. Many are professional persons. Some are church leaders. Some are business executives who have found that success in the world's eyes is not necessarily success from God's viewpoint. A few are disillusioned members of a society which has given them little real reason for living. A dramatic actress said she got her first real understanding of God at an Ashram. "I don't suppose I ever really prayed until that time," she explained. "I'd been surrounded by false values and proud people much of my life . . . and I was part of my surroundings. It was a relief to be accepted just as a person, instead of a personality." A Chicago radio script writer attending her first Ashram confessed: "I've been a Christian only three years. Before that I was an atheist. I want a time for getting close to God and for escaping a lot of the claptrap in Western religions. And I've been fighting myself so much of my life it's good to feel at peace."

There are no age barriers. Families often spend their vacation time at Ashrams and there is something for everyone. The youth learn from older people and the older participants absorb the contagious enthusiasm of the children and youth. There are no race, class or professional barriers. Although many professional persons attend the Ashrams, none are recognized by professional titles. They are no longer doctors, professors, ministers or educators. They are just known as "Brother John" and "Sister Mary." There are no barriers between those who do manual labor and those who do not. Every Ashram has its daily work period and every participant carries his or her share of the daily work load. College presidents and day laborers work side by side to the mutual benefit of each.

Ashram schedules are relaxed and informal. Silence and personal meditation are important aspects of the program. Outstanding Bible scholars lead worship and study sessions in the mornings. An evangelist brings both challenge and inspiration in morning and evening addresses. Afternoons are given over to rest, recreation and fellowship. Tennis, softball, golf and swimming are popular pastimes. Music is an important part of the total program. Prayer groups are also an integral part. A small number of persons meet together each day with the emphasis on actual prayer time, not on discussion of prayer. A prayer vigil is maintained around the clock in shifts of one hour each for the entire period the Ashram is in session. Everyone participating is urged to sign up for at least one of the hour-long sessions.

While group discussion is profitable, the person-to-person conversations that take place are, for many individuals, the high point of their experience. In these busy times the opportunity for leisurely conversation is limited. Ashrams provide ample time for meaningful conversations to take place and for the sharing of problems as well as joys. Personal counseling with competent leaders is arranged if requested. The Ashram participants desert the pressures, deadlines and confusion of their daily lives for a period of restorative peace in an attempt to "let God come in."

For Sister Anna, attendance at an Ashram had one primary motivation: "a long look at God and yourself." For eighteen years she served as the official hostess for a number of the early Ashrams held in the United States. As the movement grew and Ashrams were conducted over the entire nation she served as the Bible teacher in four to six Ashrams each year. For her, the experiences were not only a time to feed others spiritually but a time to *be* fed.

The Ashram story is one of changed lives, of movement toward the radical discipleship demanded by the Master. It has made a special impact on many who have become disillusioned with the institutional church. Described as a place to "recharge run-down batteries," a "vacation with a difference," a "healing of love to the body, mind and spirit," the only qualification for membership is that you "come as you are, but that you want to be different, to be the persons that God wants you to be."

E. Stanley Jones, the great missionary statesman and founder of the movement, died in 1973 but the Ashrams continue to grow and expand. One enthusiastic member declared: "This Ashram fellowship holds! It is rooted in God and hence is permanent." He must have been right, for now the movement has taken on an international aspect with Christian Ashrams conducted in many nations throughout the world.

The past twenty years have seen a proliferation of similar types of spiritual retreat groups. Some meet for only a short period of time, such as the *Women Aglow*, *Women Alive* and *Winning Women* fellowship study groups. All are dedicated to the concept of spiritual growth through personal meditation and sharing in small groups. Anna has been a much-sought-after speaker at many of these meetings due to her activity with the Ashram movement.

One of the more beautiful of her experiences in recent years stemmed from a Camp Farthest Out retreat. This movement was instigated by Glenn Clark in the thirties and is still drawing a number of participants each summer. In her eighty-eighth year, Anna was serving as a leader in one of these retreats which included a number of teenagers. One of the final Bible study sessions centered around the 13th chapter of John which depicts the last supper Jesus had with his disciples. The youth were not familiar with this passage, and many found themselves both surprised and awed by the startling role of servanthood Jesus demonstrated when he girded himself with a towel and knelt to wash the feet of his disciples, one by one. They were intrigued by his willingness to demonstrate the value of humility in this concrete and symbolic fashion. They were especially challenged by his statement which followed the act:

> Then if I, your Lord and Master, have washed your feet, you also ought to wash one another's feet. I have

set you an example: you are to do as I have done for
you. In very truth I tell you, a servant is not greater
than his master, nor a messenger than the one who
sent him. If you know this, happy are you if you act
upon it. (John 13: 14-18, NEB)

One of the members of the group suggested to their leader that they have such a service at the conclusion of the retreat with the teenagers washing the feet of their parents. Like many teenagers, some had feelings about their parents that were not altogether loving. In some cases there was actual hostility because of past misunderstandings. The youth felt this could be an act of real forgiveness, and the beginning of a totally new and understanding relationship with their parents.

When the youth discovered that Sister Anna was a member of a Christian denomination that had practiced the feetwashing service since its beginning in the midseventeen-hundreds they had many questions for her. How was it practiced? Why? Did it really mean anything to the persons participating? Wasn't it embarrassing to have somebody kneel down and wash your feet? Anna found herself explaining the symbolism of the service to the most excited and attentive audience she had ever encountered. And so, with her help and guidance, the service was arranged.

All parents wishing to participate were seated on the front row at the final worship service. Following the service of worship, the chapter from John was read with some explanation. And then the teenagers came, one by one, to kneel and wash the feet of their parents in response to the Christ's injunction. The heartwarming climax came for Sister Anna when a stalwart, seventeen-year-old young man came and took her by the hand, led her to the front and announced to those present: "I want to wash Sister Anna's feet." And he did. Surely the saints of heaven must have rejoiced at the amazing grace of *that* splendid scene!

This spontaneous gesture of love from a young man was symbolic of one of the most important aspects of Anna's role as a spokesperson for God. It was the warmth and esteem in which children and youth have held her for more than half a century. She has had a lifelong affinity for the young. Possibly this is a carry-over from her own childhood and youth when she substituted as a "little mother" to sisters and brother and nieces, nephews and cousins. Babies, small children, adolescents and older youth—all were drawn to her like bees to a blossom. Among her most treasured letters are those from children in whose homes she had been a guest. The large pocketbook she carries always contains small gifts for children. Miniature stuffed Koala bears, tiny dolls, small books, a bit of hard candy—here is always some little surprise, some bit of treasured trivia to keep just because it is bestowed with the love of Anna.

One little girl in whose home Anna was a guest during a spiritual retreat wanted to be sure that Anna remembered her, too. Her letter of love was decorated artistically with the colorful stamps she had received as a gift from Anna. In inch-high block letters she printed: "Dear Anna, We were so glad you were here. I want you to come back. I love you so please come back. These stickers will make you remember me."

A little boy prepared a love letter straight from the heart. It was so candid it might have been almost too much if his grandmother had ever seen it. On the front of a folded piece of construction paper the color of strawberry ice cream he had drawn a large red tulip which was carefully overlaid with some dried flowers and weeds. The message on the outside, printed in grassy green crayola stated: "All of us love you—from Philip." The uninhibited message inside stated: "We love you. We like what you had to say to us and you are better than my Grandma and you are greater." The chances are very good that Philip's Grandma would have agreed with this frank appraisal even though she did come off second. Nothing so fills Anna with joy as having the love of small children, because in her own words: "There's no pretense with small children. They know you for what you *really* are!" Their accolades can be depended upon.

Letters to Anna from teenagers were more serious. One fourteen-year-old wrote: "Please pray for me to find

God's will for my life." Another letter, signed by forty-one high school and college youth ended with: "We appreciate the spirit that you've imparted to us, and the growth that is resulting in ourselves. God bless you!" This letter followed a weekend retreat in a local church. Anna had found the youth eager to talk about God, about their contributions to the world and about what it means to really love other persons.

One of her greatest attractions for youth is the fact that with her they can *be themselves*. They can say what they feel—and they do—knowing that it will be heard in love and interpreted with understanding. One young girl, a pastor's daughter, wrote a four-page letter revealing not only how she felt about a lot of things but demonstrating a great deal of perception about current living. Among other things she wrote:

> I complained about the worship service until Father told me to write my own. So I did. I found out how difficult it is. Therefore, this will be my one and only effort. Father says he will use it when he is ready to retire. I will stay home and start packing. But it says what I wanted it to say.
>
> Also, I outlined six sermons on the life of Jesus. For some strange reason this series was not received by the preacher with wild enthusiasm. The first sermon is entitled: "They Wrapped Him in Swaddling Clothes Because they Didn't Have Pampers." The sermon on miracles is called: "What did you Expect—Kool Aid?" Actually these sermons are half serious and half tongue-in-cheek. And much better unpreached.

The young girl's letter was not entirely facetious. The closing paragraph revealed the depth of her pain for the world into which she had been born. It must be the feeling shared by many youth as they struggle to find their own place in such a world.

> World problems seem so enormous. So much suffering, much of which could be eased. Power never brings compassion. One feels so helpless and stupid. I

just get frustrated and very angry. The answers seem so obvious and simple. I guess I am naive and innocent. Politics and economics and greed complicate what should be indisputable action. The enormity of the whole thing paralyzes me. I can't help wondering how God can stand it.

Dozens of such letters written by youth to Anna reiterated this same sense of frustration, of helplessness in a world which they had no part in creating—a world in which they felt so little of the agape love demonstrated by Jesus the Christ. They could pour out their pain and anger to Sister Anna, knowing that she would understand.

The youth didn't only write letters; they went to see Anna. There were frequent letters and telephone calls requesting time to "talk things over" with her. One young man driving from a state in the deep South to his wedding in the North assured her he would stop by for a few hours if she could possibly spare the time for him. Another young girl asked for a few hours to talk after writing to Anna about some of her problems. Faced with pressures in a new job which she felt unable to handle, she concluded her letter with:

> I confess that knowing you and Baxter, Anna, whose lives have been rich and full of God's grace, who seem perpetually young in spirit, creates in me a hunger to know more about that God-centered life. But the hunger for sex, for recognition, and for a multitude of adoring friends, also creep in. My hunger for the God-filled life must not yet be great enough, else the disappointments of lesser hungers would not hurt so much, do you think?

The young persons who came to Anna were legion but probably none of their lives touched her so deeply as that of Mike Hoal. Mike was a young man in Anna's and Baxter's home church. Growing up in the turbulent sixties and seventies he, like many others of his age, became disillusioned with the church as he understood it. Under the loving guidance and total acceptance of Anna he came back into the church fellowship. He chose to temporarily leave a promising business career in order to give two years of his life in the Brethren Volunteer Service (BVS) program.

Mike and another young friend decided to drive to California for a short vacation before going into BVS. While there they spent much of their time riding the surf at San Diego Beach. Near the end of their vacation time, Mike's surfboard was caught by an unexpected wave and he was dashed up on the beach with a broken neck and other internal injuries. Quick action on the part of his companion and a lifesaving crew saved his life, but only temporarily.

When members of his family reached his bedside in California they found Mike mangled in body but not in spirit. He could not speak but he was totally conscious and could respond to family members by smiling and moving his eyes. The prognosis from the hospital physicians was devastating. Mike was hooked up to four machines, all four of which were imperative to sustain life at that point. Due to the extent of the internal injuries there was no evidence that his body could recover to where his vital organs would ever function on their own.

When faced with the desolate outlook and the highly charged, emotional decisions that had to be made, the family's first thought was of Anna. They knew of her love for Mike. They called her in Virginia and within hours she was on her way to California.

The following week Anna stood before a large group of Mike's family and friends who had come to share in a memorial service for him. She gave this brief message. It came from the heart. It went to the hearts of those who heard.

> I was out of touch with Mike for a number of years until a year ago when he created a new bathroom for us out of a closet. We soon had many visits around the kitchen table. After his work for us was finished he continued to drop by every week. One of the great challenges of my life was learning to know Mike. He had been disillusioned about some things in the institutional church. Still he accepted me, even though he knew my life was spent for the church.

Whatever doubts Mike had, I found, were honest doubts. He belonged to a generation of youth who wanted reality. I believe with Tennyson that "there is more faith in honest doubt than in half the creeds." My only concern was that I would never push him back in his search for truth. Then last summer one evening he came and rather hesitantly said: "I've been thinking about God, but I am ashamed to come to Him when I am helpless." I assured him we all come that way, recognizing our human helplessness. Then we had our first real talk about God.

Mike had an unusually kind heart. He seemed to have an antenna out to find people in need. I found he gave new courage to many. In helping others he was helped in his own problems. So he grew in an understanding of God's love.

When I first saw Mike in San Diego, I was heartbroken at the sight of his broken body, but after my first visit with him I marvelled at his response to the love of God. His body was broken and dying but his spirit was whole. When the time came for me to leave, I went to say farewell to him. He was not thinking of death but new life coming, and I said: "Mike, you have many wonderful surprises coming. You will meet the Lord face to face before I do. Please give Him my love." Mike smiled through his swollen lips and moved his eyes. I know he has carried my message.

I understand that the last message he gave family and friends present was: "I am going to be free. Go out and CELEBRATE."

So, today we celebrate with Mike. We renew our commitment never to waste the love of God.

Three years later a new swimming pool was dedicated in Mike's memory at Camp Bethel, the church camp which had been a primary project for Mike and his family for many years. Inspired by members of his family and by Anna, many more friends contributed their resources to build the pool. For years to come, thousands of children, youth and adults will celebrate the joy of living because Sister Anna helped Mike discover the joy of loving and of giving. The commitment to "never waste the love of God" was indeed realized.

Further evidence of Anna's impact as a speaker to youth is the fact that she has been invited to participate in several Church of the Brethren National Youth Conferences after she was past 80. Youth love her simplicity and directness. They appreciate the fact that she permits them to doubt, to raise questions they would not dare raise with their parents or with some other church leaders. They love her because she loves *them* and they know it.

"You are absolutely the first old lady I have ever met that gave me the desire to grow old," wrote one enthusiastic admirer. "The most wonderful thing about you is that I never thought of you as 'old.' I am sure the joy of the Lord is in your strength because you seem to have more than your share of both." This Lord to which Anna invites them is her strength—and her joy, too. He is not a stuffy, legalistic "you'd better do this or else" kind of God to which some of them have been exposed. Rather, he is the master of exploration, of excitement. He makes demands, stern ones: the cross, servanthood, forgiveness, prayer for one's enemies. Youth can identify with these stern demands.

Her speeches to youth are spontaneous and filled with humor. There is a good balance between theology and ethics, between the mystical and the practical. After the 1978 National Youth Conference at Estes Park, Colorado, Dave McFadden, the conference coordinator, wrote Anna: "While the week for most will be remembered as a whole, your role touched the lives of many in a very special way. For them, the week will be important because of your participation . . . I appreciated your rapport with the youth, and felt that you were well received. Many I spoke with named 'Sister Anna' as the highlight of the week."

Some youth were honest enough to admit, however, that they had first come to hear her under the pressure of parents who thought she was someone rather special. One surprised teenaged boy wrote her: "Hey, man, you're as great as my dad said you were!" Another wrote after a visit in Anna's home while a student in college: "Thanks for sharing your home and hospitality . . . Asha keeps telling me what a 'brain' you are but I say you're all HEART!"

When asked to what she attributed her success with youth she replied: "I begin with them where they are. I don't talk down to them. I speak to their deepest need—the need to find meaning in life, a reason for living. Finally, I love them and they know it!" It is a simple formula. And it works.

Youth have a descriptive phrase for the warm, lovely, unexpected happenings in life that bring joy. They describe such as "warm fuzzies." A warm fuzzy could be simply a squeeze of the hand in understanding, a sincere compliment for a task well performed, an unexpected telephone call or a note from an old friend. All of these little bits and pieces of reaching out to touch each other in love are warm fuzzies. Although Sister Anna had many such happenings in her later years, the one which she would never forget came on her 83rd birthday, July 30, 1976.

It was at the Church of the Brethren Annual Conference in the Civic Center at Wichita, Kansas. On that Friday evening, after three busy days of serious speechmaking and business sessions, a concert was scheduled by Andy and Terry Murray. Known among the youth as the "Brethren Balladeer," Andy had composed a number of songs about the Brethren heroes of past years, all of which lifted up the spiritual values cherished by the members of his faith: the simple life, service to humanity, pacifism, learning to love as Christ loved. All of these virtues espoused by the Brethren provided a challenge to him for "song-making." Some of these songs had become a part of many youth retreats and youth conferences with Terry at the piano and Andy playing his guitar.

Near the end of their concert on that evening, Andy announced they needed some help with several of their numbers. Within moments about four hundred and fifty children ranging in ages from four to thirteen joined them on the stage. They had been rehearsing with the musicians for the past four days and now they were ready for their big moment. It was announced that someone in the audience was celebrating an 83rd birthday. It was not until the seven thousand persons in the audience joined in singing the happy birthday song that Anna realized they were singing to *her*. After another song by the children, Andy announced that the children had a special birthday gift for Sister Anna. It was her very own song, written about her and now to be sung for her by the children, grandchildren and great-grandchildren of hundreds of her former students, co-workers and friends.

It was a moving moment, not only for Anna but for all who participated—and all did participate before the song was finished. Andy and Terry alternated in singing the verses, the children joined in with each chorus, and on the final chorus the entire audience joined in. It was a rhythmic outpouring of loving appreciation to this one who had touched the lives of so many of the thousands who were there on that unforgettable evening. At the conclusion there was a standing ovation and tumultuous applause as Sister Anna was led to the stage to receive a dozen red roses from Patricia Helman, the wife of the conference moderator, A. Blair Helman. It was Anna's moment. Her response was typical: "All that I am I owe to the Lord Jesus Christ."

This "warm fuzzy" has come back to her again and again in subsequent years. The song was later recorded by Andy and Terry and it became a regular feature at many youth meetings. As Anna expressed it: "Andy's song paved the way for me to learn to know a whole new generation of Brethren children and youth that I may not have reached otherwise." The song was sung to her by many groups on numerous occasions and one older couple even had it played at their wedding! They credited her with bringing them together in matrimony after each had lost a former mate. Since Anna could not attend their marriage her presence was felt by the playing of "her song."

SISTER ANNA, BEAUTY QUEEN

Front: Some say that beauty's only as deep as the skin,
And it's a quality that's just not relevant for men—
But though I'm of the masculine gender

I've got an opinion I'd like to render—
The loveliest person that I've ever known
Has a beauty I'd like to call my own . . .

Chorus: Sister Anna, beauty queen,
Your picture's in a magazine,
A hole in your stocking and a pocket full of
    dreams, seventy or seventeen,
The beauty-fullest person that I've ever seen.

Verse I: She's a little too short for the
High-fashioned world,
And a little too old for a jet set whirl—
But she's a real Ms. Universe at heart
Cause her heart's so big
The universe is just a part of . . .

Verse II: If you're down and feelin' kind of blue
And the hard part of life seems just the gettin'
    through,
Say "hello" to Anna, she can make you whole
'Cause her laugh's so big, (Yes, her laugh's so big)
It could cure your soul . . .

Chapter 9
"Talking on Paper"

Good speakers do not necessarily make good writers. Writing is a lonely craft and the discipline required is not always welcomed by those who need the stimulus of persons to be at their best. The fact that Anna Beahm Mow has become a highly respected and successful creative writer after she was past the age of sixty-five is indicative of her gifts as well as of her disciplined lifestyle.

"I never had any desire to write a book," Anna stated emphatically in discussing her role as a writer. "Every one of my books was requested by book editors of four different publishing houses, and I really didn't *want* to write any of them." For one who had never dreamed of becoming a successful author, who really didn't *want* to write, her output has been prolific. Ten published books, more than a dozen articles in journals and magazines, a drama for mission work depicting Christ as the hope of every age, several brochures on specific subjects assigned to her, and numerous short articles can be credited to this uniquely unwilling scribe.

If she didn't want to write, why did she do it? "Because someone convinced me I had some things that were worth printing, I guess," she answered with her familiar chuckle. They assured her, too, that her words on paper could be read, studied and lived by in future years if she would only take the time to put them between the covers of a book. Some circumstances related to the writing of each of her books appeared to be almost providential at the moment. Readers of religious writings were rapidly growing. Publishers were looking for writers who could portray the Christian message in a way their readers could understand.

When a book editor approached her about the

possibility of writing a book "for Christians who know they are saved but don't know they're supposed to grow," she was not only surprised but at the outset totally opposed to the idea. "I told him I didn't want to write any book because it would take all my best stories I used in my speeches," she said. The editor's idea intrigued her, however, because if any area of Christian living really excited Anna it was the importance of *growth*. She never believed in the idea that once baptism had taken place the Christian was a finished product. She saw life as an ongoing pilgrimage toward perfection with many side journeys and pitfalls along the way. Perhaps she *should* write a book!

And she did. Entitled *Say Yes to Life* (Zondervan, 1961), the book was dedicated "To those who know about being born into a new life but are puzzled by their growing pains." Apparently there were thousands who found themselves in that state because the sale of the book was surprisingly splendid for a first-time author. It was reprinted seventeen times with a special edition produced for readers in Great Britain. Nearly 50,000 copies were sold.

The book was described by Eugenia Price, who wrote the introduction, as "dynamite to 'phariseeism,' fresh air to personalities smothered in dogma, nourishment for growth-stunted souls, and a green light to the adventurous ones who dare to follow the big God of the New Testament." In the preface to the book, Anna wrote: "It isn't 'pie-in-the-sky' that we want, it is ability to meet our daily problems. We need discernment to know what is of life and what is of death in this crazy mixed-up world." Anna recognized that we have to be continuously converted all the days of our lives and her book was filled with common sense, pithy advice as to how this continuing conversion could take place.

Her second book, *Your Child from Birth to Rebirth* (Zondervan, 1963), was dedicated to the "Concerned Parents and Teachers of Children." This book was requested by the Zondervan book editor partly on the basis of the outstanding sales of her first book but also because there was a real need for a book which gave direction to parents and teachers of young children in the area of Christian education. Anna described it as a "simplification of the patterns I developed for the training of teachers in Christian education during my years of teaching at the seminary." She also admitted that much of what she learned about teaching children had been learned, like all parents have to learn, by making some mistakes with her own.

The book was filled with practical, down-to-earth suggestions for giving children a basis for developing their own faith. Anna felt strongly that children should be trained early to make their own choices and then to live by the consequences of those choices. She had seen the sad results of too many children reared in an atmosphere of authoritarian power, forced to obey an older person through means of fear or guilt. "Such children are seldom likely to grow into adults who make their choices in light of God's plan for their lives," she stated.

Anna called the period between one's birth and rebirth the "spiritual prenatal period." She wrote: "We cannot educate into faith but we can educate in preparation *for* faith.... Many educators have failed because they thought that everything depended on man's efforts; others failed because they thought everything depended on God's part in our lives. God's Word teaches us that God limited Himself in creation by giving man the power of choice. God always does His part, we must learn to do our part in responding to Him. Then the Christian educator's dilemma will be solved."

The fact that *Your Child from Birth to Rebirth* met a real need was proven by the statistical evidence. Zondervan made eighteen printings. There were translations into three different languages other than English: Varia Books of South Africa published an Africaans edition under the title of *Leef My King?;* in 1968 a German version was printed entitled *Dein Kind in Gottes Hand;* in 1974 a Spanish version was produced with the title of *VUESTRO HIJO: Del Nacimiento al Nuevo Nacimiento.* More than 78,000 copies have been sold around the world.

Her third book, *Going Steady With God* (Zondervan, 1965), grew out of an experience with a group of teenagers and their leaders at Camp Mardela, Maryland. She was in a retreat with them for a weekend and a week later she was concluding a meeting at a Maryland church which was about 30 miles away. When the altar call was given that Sunday evening by the pastor of the church, the entire Camp Mardela retreat group, including their leaders, came to the altar for rededication and reconsecration.

Following the service, the youth congregated around Anna at the rear of the sanctuary to ask questions, many of them with tears in their eyes because of the deep emotion they were feeling. "I have no trouble being a Christian at church. My trouble is on a date," said one vivacious high school student. "How can we apply the principles of Christian living to everyday problems?" asked another. Now that they had rededicated themselves to follow the Master of life more completely they were filled with questions about specific needs and problems.

Anna had already been requested by Zondervan to do another book for them but she felt that she was not yet ready to start another writing project. The experience with these youth made her realize that very little material had been written specifically to help youth grow spiritually. Like a sudden streak of lightning a question flashed through her mind: should this be her third book? The Zondervan editor was enthusiastic when she proposed the idea to him and soon she was busy again—attempting to write a book which would answer the questions of youth who were really earnest about finding a closer walk with God.

Her work resulted in *Going Steady with God,* a year of daily meditations for teenagers. Included along with the daily Bible readings, prayers and suggestions for personal meditations is guidance to youth for finding their own answers to the questions puzzling them, answers to be discovered in light of what God wanted for their lives. In some advice to them she wrote: "Read my words as you like, but God's word you must eat." She explained that one really did learn to "eat" the Bread of Life when it became important in one's life. Short essays on doubts, courtship and marriage, being different, knowing the truth, the power of the Holy Spirit and other timely topics were included.

One reviewer of the book wrote "The rich, relevant words of her essays make this a doubly nourishing book for young people. Mrs. Mow's seasoned insights as a missionary, educator and frequent leader of youth retreats reveal that she knows young people and she knows God." By 1976 the small volume had gone into its fourteenth printing and by 1982, 47,000 volumes had been sold.

The immediate success of this book caused the Zondervan editor to approach Anna about the possibility of writing a fourth book, one for parents of teenagers. It was becoming evident to those persons who worked with youth that many of the disturbed and delinquent ones were coming from family environments which helped to create their problems. "And so," Anna said, "I sat down and thought and thought. I thought about the things youth had confided in me in meetings over the past several years. I thought about the letters they wrote me and what I had observed in families to which I had been exposed. I came to the conclusion that the biggest problem that young people have is *parents who have an underlying irritation for one another.*"

It appeared the biggest challenge in writing *Your Teenager and You* (Zondervan, 1967) was to address the many problems that parents were facing as they approached their "midlife crisis" just as their children were entering puberty and struggling with their own crises. Anna explained: "Over and over and over again young people have said to me: 'My biggest problem is my parents, they don't love each other; how can I help my parents to love each other'?"

This fourth book was an attempt to address the problem of helping parents to help their children by first examining their own relationship under the scrutiny of unselfish love as demonstrated by Jesus the Christ. "I am not writing as a professional of any kind," Anna stated. "But I have learned that it is wise to accept the definition of love that Jesus lived out in all His human relationships. I would count no human relationship as impossible until God-love had been truly tried. The message of this book is as simple as that." The simplicity paid off. Three printings were made in the first year of publication and in 1975 an edition was printed in Spanish. 50,000 copies of *Your Teenager and You* have been sold to date.

Anna's name was beginning to be a recognized one in

the publishing world. Soon she was approached by the book editor of J. B. Lippincott with a request for a book written for persons over sixty. Her reply to him was that she "hadn't had time yet to think about being over sixty." She was seventy-four at the time. After giving it some thought, however, she decided to go ahead, and the result was *So Who's Afraid of Birthdays?* (J. B. Lippincott, 1969).

In her research for writing this book, Anna came to the conclusion that if people do not learn how to live before they are sixty, they will be in trouble after sixty. She believed that although the book was written for older persons it should be read by those in their forties and fifties to do the most good for later years. The book was dedicated to her father, I.N.H. Beahm, who was "still young at ninety-one," according to her.

Written in her lively and informal style, the book was filled with constructive help for those facing their later years. Loneliness, illness, feelings of uselessness and self-pity were dealt with in a positive way. She brought sensitive counsel to the millions of Americans over sixty-five whose vision of the years ahead had become clouded by the pressures of aging. Her hope and her aliveness sprang from every page.

Central to the whole theme of successful and graceful aging was her love for and her confidence in the mercy and goodness of God, and her staunch belief that eternity has its beginning here on earth. A friend of hers, Canon Bryan Green, was once asked by a college student if he believed in immortality. His reply was classic—and it expressed succinctly the philosophy of Anna's book: "I do not believe in immortality," said Canon Green, "that is a Greek idea. I believe in *eternal life* and that begins *now.*" Sister Anna added:

> Eternal life does begin now. We have "today" and we live in His presence and through strength given us by His Holy Spirit. So the shining secret is: If we are not afraid for *today* we need not be afraid for tomorrow. . . . For the man or woman who *knows* God, physical death is not even an interruption of the inner life. It is, rather, a great Setting Free.

So Who's Afraid of Birthdays was chosen for the *Christian Herald* magazine's Book of the Month Club.

The Secret of Married Love (J. B. Lippincott, 1970), was Anna's sixth book. She described it as being written for the first year of marriage so the wedding glow could become a steady fire. When a friend asked her how long it took to write the book she could honestly answer "fifty years"! It was during this period of publication that she and Baxter celebrated their fiftieth wedding anniversary at a beautiful reception given for them by their three children.

What she wrote had an air of authenticity about it. Her observations were based on her fifty years of marriage to Baxter, "who is as different from me as night is from day"; on many years of counseling with hundreds of husbands and wives; on a careful study of hundreds of books in the field of human behavior. In all of this study, however, there was an added dimension in marriage so far as Anna was concerned: a very thorough knowledge of the Bible and what *it* had to say about the making of a good marriage. Her preface stated:

> There is an open secret for true love, but it is so simple that few people find it. If you find this secret in the first glow of your love, you will close the door to disillusionments that the majority of newlyweds experience during the first years of their marriage.
>
> This love secret has been discerned and revealed by Jesus, Paul and others in the New Testament, but too often their teachings have been lambasted or ignored. Their interpretations for love and human relationships are considered impractical and irrelevant for modern marriage, and bewildered moderns wonder why they fail in love relationships.
>
> It is a thrill to find an ancient law of life, a love of love, that works in this very modern era. We've had it at our fingertips all the time, but we never took it seriously.
>
> This book is about that secret.

Dedicated to their three children, Lois, Joseph and Merrill and their children, the book did not keep its secret for long. It was widely used in home and family relationship classes within many Protestant denominations as well as in the Roman Catholic Church. A Spanish edition was published in 1972 and this was used extensively in the Catholic churches of Spain. By 1982 more than 6,000 copies had been sold.

The publication of Anna's seventh and ninth books came about as the result of a weekend preaching mission in a large church in Lititz, Pennsylvania. One Sunday morning she was asked to teach the combined youth and adult Sunday school classes. There were about three hundred persons with an age span of 14 to 88. How does one teach a Bible class for a group of that size and across that age span? It was a puzzlement!

Basing her lesson on some material she had developed for use with her seminary students, and using the blackboard as a teaching tool, she explained how the stories of the Old Testament heroes and New Testament characters must be considered in terms of the culture and age in which the individuals lived. Putting God's spiritual laws on one level of the blackboard and the manmade laws and ethics and customs on another level, Anna helped the hearers to understand how God's search for individuals throughout the centuries had evolved in different ways according to the times and culture of a specific age and place. There was a clear cut distinction between God's spiritual laws and the laws and values created by humans, between what was good for the immediate gratification of human wishes and the impact it might make on their eternal future. The bloody wars, multiple marriages and vindictive spirit which were characteristic of the Old Testament were measured against the new spirit of servanthood, of love and forgiveness as exemplified in Christ who pointed to a new Way in the New Testament. With Anna's clear interpretations, plus her thorough biblical knowledge, much of what was confusing before was easier for her hearers to understand.

Unknown to Anna, a book editor for a large publishing firm was in her class that morning. He was both fascinated and excited by her simple direct teaching as well as by the depth of her understanding of the total biblical story and how it could and should relate to the needs of people in this century. At the end of the class he came to her and announced: "You *must* put this into a book."

The book was initially published as *Your Experience and the Bible* (Harper and Row, 1973). In this book she let the Bible tell its own story, a story of God in search of man and of man's discovery of the meaning of that search. In a review of the manuscript, one writer commented:

> In her straightforward, down to earth manner, Dr. Mow turns the pages of the Bible into chapters in our own lives. The Bible mirrors us. Its reflection is a familiar one . . . . Christians of all demoninations will see themselves and their churches in Dr. Mow's discussions of the New Testament. The miracle of Jesus' humanity is inspiration for our own. The Last Supper is a lesson of servanthood. Pentecost reveals that there are no substitutes for the Holy Spirit, whether we call them 'organization,' 'planning' or just 'committees.' Cultural conflicts encountered by the early church in the Gentile world are very much part of today's religious scene.

Much of the basic material in this book was republished in a paperback edition known as *Find Your Own Faith* (Zondervan, 1977). This edition was widely used on college campuses and in youth study groups throughout the nation. Anna's clear-cut distinction between what was "reality" and what was "mirage" in religious experiences had a tremendous appeal for youth. One perceptive reviewer wrote:

> God still reaches out to become part of our lives, just as He did in Bible times. Wherever we are and whatever our circumstances, God is with us, as He was with David, Peter and Paul.
>
> In *Find Your Own Faith,* best-selling author Anna Mow lets the Bible tell its own story. She turns the pages of Scripture into chapters in our own lives, tracing the story of God in search of man and man's individual response to the meaning of that search as he works out his own faith.

This capsule journey through the Old and New Testaments puts the Scriptures into historical and cultural perspective, placing the lives of the Bible personalities into settings of their day so we may learn from them for our day.

Because the God of history is always relevant and contemporary, His Word mirrors us and speaks to us in our present condition.

Anna dedicated the original volume to her friend of many years, Eugenia Price. "Genie," as she was affectionately known by her close friends, had been a confidante, an advisor and a warm personal friend since the years Anna had taught in Chicago. But the depth of their friendship was beyond a mere personal relationship. It was a spiritual one. Anna paid tribute to her in these words:

> To my dear friend in the Lord, Eugenia Price, whose growth in the reality of Christ Jesus continues to inspire and challenge me.

Both editions of this book were widely used. A total distribution of 13,575 copies was made during the years the book was in print.

Anna's eighth book, *Sensitivity to What?* (Zondervan, 1975), was born out of a combination of feelings: frustration, anger and pain. *Frustration* that such a useful tool as small group dynamics could be so misused that it became a destructive and dangerous one in the hands of inadequately trained leadership. *Anger* that the encounter, sensitivity and human potential group movements were so often led by persons who took such personal pride in their leadership roles that they had no recognition of the damage they were doing to other human beings. And finally, deep *pain* because of the numerous persons whose lives were being damaged by their experiences as participants in groups that were being led by these same inept leaders. The preface of the book states why the book was written:

> Not long ago within one week I learned of five "successful" ministers who had walked out on their

wives, their children, and their parishes. I was told that each one, as a result of "sensitivity group" experience, had decided that he had the right to seek "self-fulfillment." With aching heart I exclaimed, "I feel like writing a book on 'Sensitivity to What?'" I really hadn't given a thought to such an undertaking, but my comment was reported to my editor, and the next day I received a long-distance call asking for such a book. So here I am with a year of sensitivity group reading behind me, along with several months of hard thinking.

Anna had had the experience of going through an intensive three-week group dynamics training program at the National Training Laboratory, Bethel, Maine, in 1951. This had taught her the value of small groups as a means of growth. It had also alerted her to the fact that there were inherent dangers. It was not the *use* of small group dynamics that frightened her. It was the *abuse*. Her astute observations of how the movement was being used by those who did not recognize the dangers led her to a careful study of forty-six current books in the field.

After this year of study and observation of what was happening she wrote the book. "We must be free to learn from the social scientists without being mere imitators of their methods," she wrote. "I know that some of the best social scientists are people of God; my quarrel here is with *churchmen* who are mere imitators of methods and gimmicks without discernment to know what they are doing to those who look to them for guidance."

The decades of the sixties and seventies have been described as the age of anxiety. The desperate need for intimacy which was characteristic of the times caused a mushroom-like growth of "human potential" workshops where a great deal of emphasis was placed on "feelings" and the often uninhibited expression of the same. Self-disclosure was sometimes pushed to extremes, and as one wise mental health worker observed: "The person is ripped apart, and no one has time to get him together again." In a similar vein, Sister Anna wrote in regard to this excessive emphasis on the importance of "feelings":

> The secular overevaluation of feelings is especially serious because it is accompanied by an underevaluation of ultimate values and moral commitments. It perverts freedom into license and leads to the frustration of self-centeredness. It is only as a child of God that one can know real relationship by which he can understand his feelings. He then knows when and how to be sensitive to his feelings because he is growing in his sensitivity to God.... The sensitivity we need today is a sensitivity to God and the church must be responsible for representing God's sensitivity to the people.

Apparently there was a real need for her timely warning. 4,700 copies of *Sensitivity to What?* were sold. Mental health professionals and others began to echo some of the same sentiments. By the end of the seventies there began to be a fading of the fad to "tell it all." There began to be the realization that too much emphasis on feelings as an end in itself was not the way to achieve a rewarding lifestyle.

Anna's tenth book *Springs of Love* (The Brethren Press, 1979), was in one sense a compilation of the wisdom she had gained through her many years of rich and varied experiences. Written in the form of one hundred brief essays on various phases of Christian living, such as temptation, healing, anxiety, commitment, prayer, marriage and family life, it included thoughts for meditation and appropriate scriptures for reading. This one book might well be described as the essence and aura of Anna. Here she reflected her own deep-rooted and confident faith in the power of God's love as the final and fulfilling answer to all of life's complex problems. Central to each of the meditations presented was the thought that the Holy Spirit could serve as the reader's guide to action in times of stress and as comforter in times of pain. In Anna's philosophy, one's problems should first be prayed about and then turned over to God. Then, rather than barging in and forcing one's own solution on a situation, one must wait for the Holy Spirit to bring about the necessary changes. *Springs of Love* is approaching the 10,000 mark in copies sold.

The hundreds of letters Anna has received from the readers of her books includes every age level. A college student expressed the feeling of numerous youth when he wrote: "The applications you made to ministering as a responsible Christian really hit home to me. Your understanding and interpretation of the Scriptures is mind-opening and heart-awakening." Another youth wrote to say she had promised her copy of *Going Steady with God* to enough friends to keep it in circulation for six years. A mother wrote about sharing the "Mow books" with all her family: "Even Mama, aged 92, has been reading and getting sustenance from them." A woman in her forties wrote: "I am in such deep despair and that is why I am writing you.... Your books have shown me the way to let Him lead me out of the depths into bright hope." An aging woman in a nursing home who had become very cynical and critical of much "contemporary religion" wrote: "It's one of the best things I've ever read outside the Bible. I'm ordering many copies to give to people." And a professional person involved in the translation of some of the Spanish editions wrote: "We cannot cease to praise God for the wondrous insight he has given you regarding some very difficult problems. It is His doing indeed."

It was good for Anna to know how people were responding to her writing and heart-warming to receive their words of commendation. But it also produced feelings of chagrin when she could not promptly answer the dozens of questions and pleas for spiritual help. There is little time in her busy schedule for letter writing yet she feels the need to answer as many as possible. Some persons have sent book manuscripts for her review, and there were dozens who have written to raise questions about writing as a craft. Each day's mail brings a combination of bane and blessing, frustration and fulfillment.

Numerous persons referred to the simplicity of her writing. True, her writing is simple to comprehend, but it is not simplistic. She has an encyclopedic knowledge of the Bible which shows in both her speaking and her writing. And her books were not written without thorough research and careful study of other books in related fields. Before writing *Your Child from Birth to Rebirth* she went to the Library of Congress for three consecutive days, read and made notes on thirty-nine books. From these notes, her own years of experience, and material she had used in teaching at Bethany, she produced one small book. It was almost as though her prolific reading had been strained through her comprehending brain to leave the very essence, the sheer, bedrock values and truths to be put on paper. Letters from the book editors of four different publishing houses were indicative of the fact that they not only had great respect for her scholarship and professional experence as a writer but that they also considered her a warm, personal friend.

One cannot read the writings of Anna thoughtfully without recognizing that the deep channels of her life were fed from the springs flowing from the grace of God. Those springs, channeled through her, watered the dry places in the souls of her readers. She was indeed the pipeline, the instrument for carrying His grace to a multitude by way of the written word. She learned from those who before her had put words on stone, on papyrus, in the sand or on paper. Since earliest childhood she had had an appreciable exposure to both the spoken and written word. And like the parched earth soaking up a gentle rain after a lengthy drought, Anna programmed ideas, thoughts and values into that computerlike brain of hers to reproduce them later in such a fashion they had meaning for all ages.

In one sense, her books resemble the Good Book: one is not likely to get the full import on first reading. In preparation for writing this biography all ten of Anna's books were reread within two weeks. It was a spiritual discipline and an amazing revelation. Read within the context of her total lifestyle and experiences one could not help but be impressed with her wisdom, sound common sense, deep devotion to the Master and the timelessness of her writing. Much of this was missed in the initial casual reading of her books in former years.

No greater tribute to Sister Anna's ability as a writer has been made than this observation of a young Swiss woman:

> She has a happy way of talking on paper!

Chapter 10
Ambassador of God's Grace

The word *travel* has broad connotations. For some, travel is of sheer necessity and means getting from one place to another with as little inconvenience as possible. For some, travel means exciting adventure. For some, it means vacation time and a change of life's dull, daily routine. For others, it means the expansion of cultural horizons. For Anna, travel means all of these things, with an added dimension: an opportunity to share her contagious, bubbling enthusiasm and joy in living with all she meets, whether for a moment or a month.

"If the Lord hadn't blessed me with so much good news to share I could stay home more," she once quipped. Her years as a missionary in India gave her an opportunity for much traveling in that country where she learned much about the Eastern religions and cultures. She had made hundreds of trips crisscrossing the United States and Canada to serve as a leader in ashrams, camps, conferences and to address numerous other groups. She made four trips abroad to serve as a lecturer on the life and travels of St. Paul. Several trips were made to Palestine with small groups of persons who benefited greatly from her thorough knowledge of Bible history and the culture of the lands visited. Nowhere has Anna had the opportunity for being her Maker's ambassador so much as in her travels. Though she never in her life owned an automobile, very few of her contemporaries could equal her record for the number of miles traveled.

She has all the assets of a good traveler: adaptability, an insatiable curiosity about people, places and modes of living. She also has a profound respect for human dignity and the culture of every country she visits. Those who travel with her discover that her keen sense of humor is at its sharpest when she is in group situation where having fun is not only appropriate but the major objective. Whenever a small group is clustered together with a lot of happy laughter it is safe to assume that Anna is in the middle of it all. Although she has lived a serious life in terms of hard work and application to what she perceives to be her calling from God, she recognizes the need for ministering to oneself on occasion by just having a lot of fun. She believes in a well-balanced life, and travel for her is a time for fun, for fellowship and for growth.

Whenever she was at home there were stacks of unanswered mail facing her, dozens of telephone calls to take, speeches to be written, books that needed reading. There was little time for real relaxation. Throughout her life she learned the art of taking the "small vacations" advocated by many psychologists and behavior specialists today. As a child her small vacations consisted of slipping off to the attic with a book or magazine to read. As a busy mother, missionary and teacher she took time out for listening to good music and going to art shows. Her travels in later years provided her with the same relaxation—the opportunity to recharge her mental, emotional and spiritual batteries. One who knew her well sent her a bon voyage note once which ended with: "Do have a wonderful trip as I know you will for you will take yourself with you." And the self she took with her was one which was truly at home in the world, no matter in what part of the world she happened to be.

Of all the travel experienced by Anna and Baxter none was so rewarding as a return to India for a two-month visit. It was like going home—home to where their children were born, home to where so many dear friends still lived and home to where the two of them had discovered much of life's real meaning.

They left Dulles International Airport on the evening of November 15, 1965. Three of Anna's sisters, their son Merrill and his wife Kathy, and seven of their "darling grandchildren" came to see them off. Three days with the Society of Brothers north of London gave them an opportunity to see many interesting sights there and to enjoy the rich fellowship of the group that had been such an important part of Merrill's life. The stay there was especially rewarding for Baxter since it gave him an opportunity to return to Oxford University and walk through the halls at Jesus College where he had studied more than fifty years before.

The next stop was in Beirut, Lebanon where daughter Lois and her family had lived for three years while her husband, Ernie, taught at the American University. When they arrived in Bombay, November 23, at 4:30 a.m., the custom officials did not require them to open their luggage for inspection. They did, however, ask for the serial numbers of their traveler's checks and for the exact amount of cash they were bringing into the country. "I had to dig into an inside pocket below my chin, right in front of the officer! But there is no false modesty in India," wrote Anna. Their time in Bombay was spent with two couples, the Yogendras and Jack and Lila McCray. The Yogendras were friends of their Chicago years who were now operating a Yoga Institute and a modern research and health therapy center. The McCrays were directing the Church of the Brethren mission program located at the south end of Bombay.

Anna and Baxter weren't the only visitors to Bombay that week. Pope Paul XIII came, too, along with 100,000 other visitors from all over the world. They had come to celebrate the worldwide Eucharistic Congress. From the fifth floor of the McCrays' apartment the Mows had a panoramic view of the sea as well as the thousands of poor villagers who had walked to Bombay for the Congress. The pilgrims camped in the park and at the seashore nearby. The Mows watched the preparation of the beautifully decorated platform which was erected to seat the important foreign dignitaries as well as the standee stalls for another 250,000 persons.

"The Pope made a very good impression on India," Anna wrote later."He did exactly the right things to win India's heart .... The government put out a special stamp for the occasion. It did not choose St. Exavier but chose St. Thomas for the stamp. This emphasized to all India that

Christianity was not a 'foreign religion'—it was in India long before it was ever heard of in Northern Europe or in America."

Pervin, the foster daughter for whom Baxter and Anna had provided financial support for many years, came to Bombay to see them and this was one of the brightest spots of their entire visit. Lois had given her mother some money to buy things for her with the advice to have fun shopping. "I never had more fun shopping," wrote Anna later. "Pervin always went with me. There are many new shops with controlled prices, and so there is no need for haggling as we did 25 years ago. The beautiful silks, woolens, woodwork, ivory, cottons and crafts of all kinds give one a breathtaking and mouthwatering experience. Much of the time I just looked, but Oh! what fun!"

After a day in Ankleshwar and two days in Ahmedabad visiting with Indian friends and the missionaries serving these two stations, the Mows went to New Delhi for four days. Their hosts there were the Cliff Robinsons. Robinson was serving as the director for the International Council for Christian Leadership, an interdenominational organization which promotes Christian activities around the world. "The work they are doing in India is thrilling indeed, and so relevant to the present needs," a grateful Anna wrote to her family and friends.

The visit in New Delhi also provided an opportunity for spending some time with Madame Pandit, a dear friend since the days their children had been in school together at Woodstock more than thirty years before. Although she and Anna corresponded through the years and Mrs. Pandit had visited the Mows in the United States, it was the first opportunity for again seeing her in India and hearing firsthand about all of the many changes which had come about politically since the death of Gandhi. "Nan," as she was affectionately called by Anna and other close friends, was now a member of the Indian Parliament where she replaced her brother, Jawaharlal Nehru, who had died the previous year. Through a request by Madame Pandit, the Mows had the privilege of observing a session of the Parliament. They also visited the Prime Minister's House, which had been turned into a memorial to Nehru, as well as the cremation sites of both Gandhi and Nehru. Having personally observed the great strides which India had taken under the leadership of these two statesmen, it was an awe-inspiring privilege to visit those places made sacred by their deaths.

Excerpts from a letter Anna wrote to her family and friends give a picture of what this journey meant to them:

> We had two weeks in Bulsar, our last home in India. We visited nearly every Christian home in that large community. We had side trips to Bilimora, Khergam, and our old home at Jalapor for a betrothal ceremony, then another jeep ride with Laura Sewell for four days in Vyara. The Vyara days will be remembered especially for the visit with Dhirajbai, whose childhood story I have told to hundreds of children; and for Jumnabai, who was matron of the girl's school when we lived there in 1923-25; for the agricultural research station where Japanese specialists are helping India grow more rice; for the labors of the Indian pastor there as well as the work in the surrounding villages.
>
> We returned to Bulsar for Christmas and New Year. Again we had Indian dinners everywhere. These meals were like a sacrament, especially when they gave us rice. The food shortage because of the poor crops last year had hit everday living. One family's ration of rice for a month is what they formerly ate in one day! Prices of food staples range from three to ten times as much as last year, but salaries have not increased! So every meal with these dear people was a love meal.
>
> Christmas morning in Bulsar was like Easter Sunday in America. The church was decorated and everyone came—in best clothes. After an inspiring service, Pastor Philemon told of the need for a new wing to the church. The people stood up one after another and said how much they would give. Out of their *living* they promised to give over Rs 4000. (The Pastor's salary is only Rs 155 per month—less than $30.)
>
> Our last day of two wonderful months arrived. Some twenty of our dear Bombay friends came to see

us off in old Indian style at midnight of Jan. 13-14. By 3 p.m. of that very long day we were in New York.... So many of you took part in this wonderful experience of ours and we thank everyone. Merry Christmas, Happy New Year and Joyous Easter which brings the only hope for this crazy world.

Anna's most exciting trip and a real fairy-tale travel adventure began with a letter she almost threw in the trash. Shortly after returning from a three-week tour of Palestine, Greece and Italy with her daughter in the summer 1966, she was going through a mountain of mail that had accumulated in her absence. Among the letters was one from New York dated August 15, 1966. It stated simply:

Dear Mrs. Mow:
Congratulations!
    We have just been advised by the judges that you have been awarded the Grand Prize in the *Ladies Home Journal* International Fashion Label Sweepstakes which consists of a trip to New York, Paris, London, Rome and return. Your prize consists of round-trip transportation, hotel accommodations and meals for two people and may be taken anytime within one year from the date of this letter.
                      Yours truly,
                      Richard Kane
                      Ex. V. Pres. Marden-Kane, Inc.
                      Contest Services

At first she was sure the letter was a promotion scheme of some type. She was ready to throw it in the trash along with other "junk" mail. However, a second and then a third reading made her think she should at least inquire what it was all about. She had entered no contest that she could recall and had no recollection of any contact with the *Ladies' Home Journal* except for the fact she had recently renewed her subscription. And of all things she wasn't interested in it was visiting all the fashion houses of Europe. That *was* a joke—she, who had made or made over most of her own clothes since she was fifteen years old! It had to be a hoax.

Inquiry proved that it not only was no joke but that it would be a thirty-day trip with all expenses paid plus a generous allowance for extras and special fashion shows for her and her guest at *Saks, Fifth Ave., N.Y.; Givenchy's, Paris; Patou, Florence; Dior, Rome* and *Molyneaux, London.* It couldn't be! But it was.

Baxter had little interest in being part of a fashion show tour so he suggested that daughter Lois go in his stead. Anna had a real hesitancy about asking Lois because they had only recently returned from the trip to Palestine. A call to Ernie and Lois in Mexico set her mind at ease. This was an opportunity that was too fantastic to turn down. Of course she could go. The time was set for mid-June, 1967, just as soon as Lois was through with her teaching job in Mexico.

By early May, 1967, Anna's schedule of speaking and writing had been rearranged and soon the tickets for their trip arrived along with a detailed itinerary. There were also tickets for some entertainment features along with sufficient money to cover any side trips they might choose to take away from the major cities. With the arrival of all this bounty they were finally convinced that the trip was not a dream—and that there were no gimmicks.

Now that they were sure it was going to happen, Anna wrote a letter to the *Journal* thanking them and also explaining what an important role the magazine had taken in their family.

> This award is of special significance to me because I was raised on *Ladies Home Journal.* My mother was your oldest living subscriber for a number of years. You sent it to her free for awhile because of that. She began her subscription the first year the *Journal* was published. Mr. Curtis, Edward Bok, Mrs. Rohrer, the Country Contributor, etc., were our family friends.

Not wanting those who were providing the trip to believe that fashionable clothing was a consuming passion of her life, Anna closed her letter with this candid confession:

We will be delighted with the fashion shows in New York and other cities which you are planning for us, but we would be frightened if we were under obligation to buy $500 dresses, for my husband and I live on Social Security and a little more and my daughter teaches school and has two daughters in college!

This frank admission may have been the reason for another unexpected and unbelievable happening. Shortly after their arrival in New York on June 22, 1967, a letter was delivered to Anna at their hotel. Lois had gone out with a friend a short while and here is her vivid account of what happened on her return:

When we got back to the hotel we found mother beaming as she told me to sit down for she had received another letter, delivered in person, along with two gorgeous yellow orchids. I hadn't had an orchid in I couldn't remember when and I just sat there admiring it while mother started reading the letter. It was my turn to scream, and the tears trickled down my cheeks. Surely it was Cinderella happening to us . . . . I didn't come down out of the clouds for a month but this was really a high point.

The letter was from Pat Tregellas, promotion manager at the *Journal*. It announced that there was to be a special fashion show for them the next morning at Saks, Fifth Ave. And furthermore, "as part of your prize you may select a $750 wardrobe from Sax for either your daughter or yourself." For a little girl who had loved beautiful things all of her life but whose clothes as a child were often "made-overs" and as an adult were often "make-dos," this had to be the answer to an impossible dream!

They had 24 hours to plan for the spending of this unexpected bounty. But there wasn't much time for dreaming or planning. There was lunch at New York's famous Act I Restaurant and dinner at the Top of the Six's with a cousin of Anna's. This was a delightful prelude to seeing Mozart's *Magic Flute* at the new Metropolitan Opera House at Lincoln Center. Lois, who taught art in school, was almost as much thrilled by the original Chagall paintings hanging in the lobby and the beauty of the priceless Austrian chandeliers hanging there as she was by the opera performance. "Since Mother and I are both opera buffs, we relished every minute of it and were sorry when it was over. Back at the hotel we tried to calm ourselves enough to go to sleep. Mother succeeded long before I did," she wrote. In all the excitement of the day they had not forgotten that 22 years ago they were preparing for the most important event of Lois's life—her wedding. Her 22nd wedding anniversary coincided with the date of their departure for Europe.

Characteristic of both of them, they decided to share the benefits of the next morning's special shopping spree. First they chose gifts for their family members. Shirts and shorts were selected for the men and three lovely knit dresses for the daughters of Lois. Then came their own choices. For Lois, a dress with matching coat of navy blue accented with light green checks, a two-pieced bright wool suit and a basic black dress with a long waist and pleated skirt made of Jersey Banlon. Anna chose a lined jacket dress in a navy print made of French silk and a dinner dress of shirred silk chiffon plus a noncrushable silk ribbon hat that would be eminently useful for her many traveling dates. Five pairs of shoes for the two of them completed their major purchases with enough money left over to buy some lovely pearl earrings and several pairs of hose. There was a final gift for each of them: a handsome gold pin inscribed with the admonition to "never underestimate the power of a woman!" Little did those fashion experts realize that they were pinning their message on one who at 74 years of age knew so well what real power and real womanliness were all about!

After lunch with Ms. Tregellas, Anna returned to the hotel to rest in preparation for their evening flight to London. Lois went to the *Journal* editorial offices where she spent several hours with the pattern and sewing editor who explained in detail how these pages of the magazine were produced for each issue. After her return to the hotel they repacked their bags and arranged to have the family gifts and some of their clothes shipped home. Later that afternoon they were ready to leave on their big adventure.

It is doubtful if the sights and sounds of Europe were ever enjoyed by two more appreciative or astute individuals than these two. Both of them had a love for and an extensive knowledge of music, art, and architecture. The years Lois had spent in Lebanon and Mexico had given her an above-average interest in the field of archaeology. Her participation in several digs had increased her fascination for the patterns of living that were being uncovered by this important science in the study of human history. Both had been ardent students of history and both had more than a passing interest in the development of political, religious and economic structures in past and present civilizations.

Each of them had had a fleeting glance of some of the European cities when passing through on assignment to some other place. And it was always under the limitation of both time and travel budgets that did not permit seeing the many things which they knew so much about but had little opportunity to enjoy. With no worries about how their travel would affect the family budget, with the new clothes provided by the *Journal* as well as all of the many other extras so thoughtfully provided, all they had to do now was enjoy, enjoy. And enjoy they did!

Five days in London were appreciated to the utmost. Settled in the lovely Westbur Hotel, where, in addition to all the other elegance the lobby boasted a half dozen new fresh flower arrangements daily, they absorbed the ambience of this romantic and courageous old city. They were there when the season was at its loveliest. With rose trees blooming everywhere and a profusion of colorful flowers in the gardens of the quaint little English cottages and public parks, the outdoor scenery was as picturesque as a travel folder.

They saw many of the traditional tourist's "musts": Trafalgar Square over which Lord Nelson on his Pillar rules with the thousands of pigeons that keep him company; the Houses of Parliament with Big Ben standing timeless guard; London Bridge of childhood memories; Fleet Street where most of London's newspapers are published and where

Samuel Johnson and Charles Dickens had their hangouts in bygone days. They visited the Tower of London where Lois declared, "You can just *feel* history here." Westminster Abbey was seen twice, once for church service on Sunday morning and again to relive its history through a guided tour. They saw the remains of Coventry Cathedral which had been almost destroyed during the bombings of World War II. The walls were left standing, though the roof, the beautifully hand-carved ceilings, the priceless stained glass windows and most of the church furnishings had been destroyed. "We were there at sunset," wrote Lois, "and it was a moving experience to see the cross before the altar made from charred timbers taken from the remains of the roof." The words "Father, forgive them" carved on the altar made the scene even more poignant as they realized more fully than ever before the futility and the senseless destruction caused by war.

They saw Madame Tussard's Wax Museum, Windsor Castle, Hampton Court with much of King Henry VIII's memorabilia, and the pomp and pageantry of the changing of the guard at Buckingham Palace. They decided after seeing the huge drafty kitchens and the great open fireplaces where the King's many banquets were prepared that cooking couldn't have been much fun there, nor easy. They also saw the Queen's Doll House, a reconstruction in miniature of the Royal Palace with all the priceless furnishings reproduced to scale. They were told that this Doll House had been a plaything of the present Queen Elizabeth when she was a child.

One of their greatest joys in London was a reunion with a friend of past years, Doris Feeny Jagadeesh. Married to a young Indian surgeon, Doris and her husband took them to play, *India, Arise,* at Moral Rearmament's Westminster Theatre. The play demonstrated the faith of young Indians in a future of peace, freedom and brotherhood. The cast of 60 had traveled 8,000 miles in India and had reached London after performing in theatres and on television in Beirut, Damascus, Nicosia, Rome, Paris, Switzerland and Holland. For Anna and Lois it was an exciting reminder of the country they both knew and loved so much. The message of peace and brotherhood also made an impression on the drama critic of the *South Wales Evening Post.* He wrote:

> A polished, fast moving show with great depth and feeling. It is an expression of a new spirit rising in a nation uniting people where so much pulls them apart .... It is a product of passion in the hearts of young Indians. The passion is to bring about a change in our country and the world.

On another night the two of them saw one more play together, the toe-tapping *Hello Dolly.* Lois went alone on another evening to see Anna Neagle in *Charlie Girl* and to see Shakespeare's *Midsummer Night's Dream* in Regent Park. With the ancient, outdoor setting much as it was during the lifetime of Shakespeare, the only reminder of the 20th century was an occasional airplane overhead.

June 30th found the travelers in Paris at the new Paris Hilton Hotel which boasted: "In Paris you can't miss us. We have a rather large steel sculpture in our front yard," referring to the Eiffel Tower a block away. On their second night there they had dinner at the restaurant on the second stage of the Eiffel. Lois wrote enthusiastically: "The food was delicious, the sunset gorgeous in pink and red and the night lights luminously romantic. What an evening!"

Sunday morning found them at the Cathedral of Notre Dame for High Mass where they rapturously soaked up good organ music and choir singing as the sun came pouring through the stained glass windows. From there they went to the American Church in Paris where they participated in communion service which ended with the singing of "My Country 'Tis of Thee." The music was not quite so glorious as in Notre Dame but it still produced goose bumps for both Lois and her mother. The fellowship afterwards with many Americans living and traveling in Paris was remembered with real joy.

The afternoon was spent at the Lourve where they both stood in quiet awe as they saw the originals of many great art masterpieces: Venus de Milo, the Winged Victory, Mona Lisa and many other old masters' paintings. They lingered and looked until the doors were closed at sunset.

In the evening, Lois took a bus out to Versaille to see the thrice-yearly Grand Night Festival, a spectacular pageant recreating the time of Louis XIV. There were dances, hunting scenes, royal coaches, parades and garden parties all taking place in and around the magnificent flower gardens and fountains surrounding Versaille. It was all intermingled with colored lights which featured the forests, fountains, actors and spectators at appropriate times. Midway during a final fireworks display a soft gentle rain began to fall, but no one seemed to mind. It was one of those magic moments when people were so caught up in the joy of participation that few of them bothered to notice they were being soaked to the skin.

The next two days were spent sightseeing in Paris and shopping along the Rue Rivoli. They also saw Paul Scofield as Sir Thomas Moore in *A Man for All Seasons,* and Lois went to the famous Paris Opera House to see a ballet.

Their next stop was in Florence, Italy, where they stayed for four days at the Villa Medici, a new and modern hotel that had been decorated in the style of the Renaissance. Located just two blocks from the River Arno and one of its most ancient bridges, the hotel had a delightful garden and their room window looked out over the back yard of a nearby convent. Here Sister Anna sat for hours enjoying the garden and watching the nuns as they worked and meditated daily in their own gardens. Several times they had dinner on the roof of the hotel where they had a marvelous view of the dome of the city's great Cathedral and the Giatto Tower.

Their "fashion day" in Florence was spent at the House of Palazzo Pucci. It was an old-fashioned palace furnished with rare and beautiful antiques. There they saw a dress that "was so lovely it looked like a rainbow," according to Anna. Lois bought a bright blouse with strong, gay colors in a geometric design. Wearing this would always bring back memories of their thrill at seeing Michelangelo's statue of *David,* of the Gates of Paradise, the Uffizie Galleries, the Ponte Vecchio with its gold-smithing shops. It would also remind them of the courage of this ancient old city which rose up to repair and restore the art treasures damaged in the great flood of November, 1966, only nine months prior to their visit.

"Florence has always been the city of artists and artisans, and in the artist lies the power of self-renewal," wrote one admirer of this amazing old city. Small wonder that when Anna was asked about their trip and the city she would like to go back to the reply was without one moment of hesitation: "It would be Florence; I found it the most beautiful, the most inspiring of all."

Six days in Rome provided an opportunity for Lois to indulge her interest in archaeology. Side trips to Pompeii and Sorrento and the excavations of Emperor Hadrians Villa and those taking place beneath St. Peter's were an exciting and educational experience for her. She had participated in enough digs to fully appreciate the complexity of the excavations as well as the historic importance of the treasures being unearthed. In describing the excavations at Hadrians' 300-acre villa where he went for his summer diversions she wrote:

> It had everything: stables, swimming pools, gardens, libraries, guest houses, banquet halls ... there were ways connecting the baths, theatres, etc., beneath the whole thing. There were also underground passages so the slaves could go from place to place and not bother the guests on the regular level.

Tours to the Panthenon, the Vatican Museum, the Sistine Chapel and St. Peters were of special interest to both Anna and Lois. Seeing the many very old musical manuscripts, the gold chalices, crosses and vestments, ancient books, sculptures, tapestries and paintings all done so many centuries ago to honor her beloved Lord was an experience that Anna would never forget. All of her life she had read and heard about the genius of Michelangelo and others of his generation, and now to stand in the presence of so many of his works was awesome.

They also had the unusual experience of seeing five bishops elevated to the status of cardinals in a special papal mass at St. Peters. Part of the three-hour ceremony included the shaving of the head of each bishop. When three of them turned out to be shiny bald, both Lois and her mother were puzzled to know what would be done for them. They needn't have worried. The problem was solved by giving the heads of each of the three bald bishops a good scrubbing! During this special mass the Pope was carried down the aisle by sixteen young men all dressed in bright red uniforms. "The Pope has a practice of meeting the people's eyes as he goes along blessing them," Lois wrote later, "and he caught both Mother's and mine. It was quite a thrill."

Two glorious evenings were spent at the Baths of Caraculla, an ancient ruin which had been unearthed and was now fixed up as a huge open-air theater for operatic and dramatic presentations. In this setting they saw two of their favorite operas: *Aida* and *La Boheme*. Lois' word paintings of these were so vivid one can sense the joy and excitement these evenings brought to both of them:

> This first evening we went to see *Aida* and what an experience that was! As often as I have seen *Aida* and even when I sang with the chorus, this was something really super. Never had either Mother or I seen such staging, costumes or showmanship. There were at least 600 persons on stage during the triumphal scene, including four brown horses with mounted guards; but the most daring feat was bringing Rhadames in on a white and gilded chariot drawn by four spirited white horses! And I do mean spirited, rearing and lunging. The driver was holding on to the reins with all his might, as well as two grooms who were grasping the bridles after the horses got onto the stage . . . while the tenor sang his solo before he stepped out of the chariot. As if that were not enough, they had a camel in the Nile scene! All the singing of course was superb, but the staging was really spectacular and breathtaking.

Sound of Light was another dramatic treat enjoyed in the excavated ruins of the Roman Forum. A program of music and synchronized stereophonic lighting effects along with running comments in four different languages traced the history of Rome from its founding in 754 B.C. up through the ages to the time of Christianity. After seeing this they could appreciate more fully the impact of this immortal old city on the face of the world's passing civilizations.

A brief stay in Madrid brought their trip to a conclusion. Lois had an opportunity to compare the Mexican bullfights to those of Spain and to see some of the world's best Flamenco dancers. Together they saw the Royal Palace of Alfonso XIII and the Prado Museum where the best works of Boya, Velasquez, Murillo and El Greco were on display. On a side trip to the Toledo Damascene factory, they saw this intricate art form demonstrated. A visit to the John Deere factory near Madrid was a must for Lois since her husband had worked for this company for many years.

When interviewed by a newspaper reporter shortly after their return home, Anna concluded the interview with one of her usual direct statements: "This trip was marvelous and we enjoyed every minute of it and now I'm ready to be poor again!" It was a joyful interlude in a long and busy life but Anna had important business to finish. There was work to be done and she must be about the doing, not resting on past experiences no matter how pleasing and delightful.

For Anna, the trip did not end with their return home. She made good use of it as an illustration in many of her speeches as a parable of God's grace and gifts to us. Shortly after her return she concluding a speech by telling briefly about the trip and then saying:

> Here was this big envelope in my hand for thirty days of undreamt of pleasure—but the promise of the trip was not mine until I took the trip. I had to get on planes, go to the luxury hotels, take the tours. The promise was not mine until I accepted it in obedience to the designated plan. Never once in the thirty days did we feel irritated because the plan was made out for us. We had nothing but gratitude in our hearts for this marvelous gift. For all the thirty days, I felt undergirded by grace, even the grace of God. I had not knowing-

ly done anything to get the trip. I didn't deserve it, but it was mine for the taking. In our hands we have the word of God with all God's promises for each of us, but His grace is not ours until we take it.

I should add that my prejudiced friends said I deserved this great gift, but that cannot be. Three weeks after we returned my suitcase was stolen in Union Station in Washington, D.C., a terrible loss. If I deserved the trip, I also deserved this loss. So I know it had nothing to do with being deserved. It is because of the love and grace of God that I am what I am. And the love which he has showed me has not been wasted.

Chapter 11
The Wild Hope, the Faith Tremendous

> An endless line of splendor
> These pilgrims with Heaven for home,
> Our wild hope, who shall scorn
> That in the name of Jesus
> The world shall be reborn?
> —Vachel Lindsay

It was an interesting development, one of the small hinges of fate on which the doors of history turn, that in Anna Mow's eighties there began to be a worldwide revival of interest in the man known as Jesus, the Christ. This One, to Whom she had completely dedicated her life and in Whose Way she believed implicitly, appeared to be coming into His own in the fullness of time. For nineteen centuries, the poets, the philosophers, the priests and the prophets had pointed to the "wild hope," the "faith tremendous" that one day a new spiritual kingdom would be established, a new world would be reborn when sufficient followers were ready to subscribe to the simple but profound concepts of Christ's teachings.

Shortly after Anna's birth at the beginning of the twentieth century, the twin gods of science and industrial revolution had so excited the collective minds of humankind that man almost succeeded in becoming his own little god. Self-fulfillment, self-realization and enjoying the fruits of his own palate-teasing worldly creations became sufficient reason for living. Succeeding generations had little use for the stuffy wisdom of past centuries which had insisted that "no man is an island" and the "kingdom of Heaven is within." Individual self-centeredness led to extreme nationalism as had always been true throughout bygone centuries and bygone civilizations. This, in turn, led to continuous worldwide warfare in defense of national interests and economic survival.

By midcentury the world of nations had grown increasingly economically interdependent. A few individuals began to recognize that eventually humankind would be forced to survive as brothers, with the good of the entire world community considered, if it were to survive at all. "The world has narrowed into a neighborhood before it has broadened into a brotherhood," declared one such prophet and the statement was echoed and re-echoed by a few astute politicians.

It was at this point that the man Jesus again began to make His Presence felt to a significant degree on the world scene. It was almost as though He had been propelled from the side wings onto the center stage of life's continuing drama by the midcentury God-is-dead theological controversy. The world's flower children began to espouse His way of life, albeit unconsciously as well as untraditionally. New religions began to evolve and older religious denominations became further fragmented. Hard rock operas began to extol Christ's virtues to the deafening roar of electronic music and wildly flashing psychedelic lights. New versions of the Word of God were introduced almost annually and books about Jesus rolled from the religious presses like water over a dam. At the end of several decades of popularizing Jesus, it seemed that the more we knew *about* Him, the less we *knew* Him.

Strange ways of worship began to be experienced and the phrases "salvation of men's souls" and "born-again Christians" were heard so often and sometimes in such unlikely places that they almost became common cliches. Television and radio became popular mediums for spreading the Christian gospel, and millions of persons were reached by the printed word in the far corners of the globe.

This worldwide clamor for Christlike living created an ambivalent situation. There was confusion in the traditional denominations as to how one best discovered the mind of Christ. Many communicants within the institutional churches had not yet discovered the healing bliss of being a part of the church as the Body of Christ. Spiritual loneliness was pervasive; all too often persons felt isolated from themselves, from their fellow communicants and from God. There were differing interpretations of what it meant to be "born again." For some individuals it needed to be a dramatic and emotional spiritual experience at a specific point in time and place. For others it was simply a quiet, steadily growing knowledge that nothing in all the world could separate them from the love of God, and the realization that nothing was so important as learning to love their fellow man in that same way. For these, salvation and creation were a continuing process, a never-finished, never-ending journey toward the perfection of life as exemplified in the Christ.

It was into this cacophony of confusion and clamor that Sister Anna's continuing reminder that "Jesus is Lord" began to be heard in a new light. It was reviving music to hundreds of weary and searching world pilgrims. And during the sixties and seventies she began to be joined in this refrain by some world-recognized figures. Some of these were theologians, some were not, yet all strongly endorsed the teachings of Jesus as the only method by which the human race could hope to survive on the face of the earth.

Among this number was Barbara Ward, the noted British economist whose judgment in matters of economic development was sought by industrialists throughout the world. A political scientist of world stature, she wrote and spoke specifically of the danger of extreme nationalism in a world which had become so interdependent economically. In her book *Spaceship Earth* (Columbia University Press, 1966), she expressed words of warning but also of hope.

> Almost every major influence on a man's life today is international. His ultimate emotions and loyalties remain national. This is the gap through which our little world threatens to plunge to ruin ....

> What are the chances of the human experiment rising above these nationalist contradictions? We have all too many grounds for pessimism . . . . Man from his origins has conspicuously failed to recognize a brother in fellow human beings who happened to stand in the way of his needs or intents . . . . Quicker transport and communication makes contact across frontiers a matter of course and helps to build up communities of like-minded men and women for whom the discipline, the truth, the adventure of their field of learning far outweigh the differences of language or politics which their national origins impose.
>
> And even in faith itself, which has divided the world so bitterly, there is evidence of a new concern for unity. The ecumenical movement is above all an attempt to reach beyond the differences of the past in order to encounter the reality of a common human experience, a sense of brotherhood, if the term has not been overused, a discovery of what unites rather than divides the communities of the world . . . . It has required great vision, great holiness, great wisdom to keep alive and vivid the sense of the unity of man. It is precisely the saints, the poets, the philosophers, and the great men of science who have borne witness to the underlying unity which daily life has denied.

On a more personal and individual basis, which is what the basic teachings of Jesus are all about, Ward warned:

> Every single ancient wisdom and religion will tell you, don't live entirely for yourself. Live for other people. Think of what that means in concrete terms. Don't get stuck inside your own ego because it will become a prison in no time flat, and for God's sake don't think self-realization will make you happy. That is the way you will land in hell — your own hell . . . . Self-realization comes in going out to others, to creation, to art, to knowledge. One of the oldest truths is that he who loses his life shall find it.

Sister Anna echoed these words by Barbara Ward relentlessly, warning her hearers to avoid self-centeredness at all cost. One of her favorite authors was Dr. Fritz Kunkel, a German psychiatrist who wrote *Creation Continues*. According to Dr. Kunkel, self-centeredness was truly "condensed darkness." According to Sister Anna, it was not only condensed darkness but one of life's most subtle temptations. She had dealt with her own "dark night of the soul" and she had helped hundreds of others to deal with theirs. Again, hers was a deeply held conviction that the only way to rid oneself of "self" was to develop a personal, passionate devotion to the living Christ.

Imprisonment became a stark reality for many of Anna's contemporaries because of their defiance of the "kingdoms of this world" on behalf of the rights of those whom they served. The Mows were in India during the nonviolent revolution led by Gandhi to free India from British rule. Anna's dearest Indian friend, Madame Pandit, served several prison sentences during this time for a total of three years' imprisonment. Several of the Mows' missionary friends in China were detained in prison camps and several lost their lives there during the Chinese revolution.

During World War II, Anna worked with American Japanese Christians detained by the US government in prison camps. At this same time, she was teaching her seminary students in Chicago and a young Lutheran theologian, Dietrich Bonhoeffer, was imprisoned and finally executed on April 9, 1954, in a Nazi German concentration camp. Two of Bonhoeffer's best-known books, *The Cost of Discipleship* and *Letters from Prison,* bear striking testimony to what it meant to be a Christian in the mid-twentieth century.

Three others suffered imprisonment for their stands in behalf of human rights: There was Viktor Frankl, a victim of the Nazi war machine who survived the horrible rigors of several concentration camps to found the prestigious Neurological Poliklinik in Vienna. His book, *Man's Search for Meaning,* is a classic in its field and a clear demonstration of Nietzche's maxim that, "He who has a *why* to live can bear with almost any *how!*" There was Martin Luther King, Jr., outspoken defender of the civil rights of blacks in the US who was imprisoned on numerous occasions and finally assassinated. There was Alexander Solzheinitsyn, the Russian expatriate who was imprisoned for a long period and later awarded the Nobel Prize for Literature for his *Gulag Archepelago*.

The tragedy and senselessness of international warfare came closer to Anna when two young sons of personal friends were victims of the machinery of militarism. Ted Studebaker, a college student from Ohio, was shot in Vietnam while there doing alternative service as a conscientious objector to war. On July 13, 1982, another young college friend, 20-year-old Enten Eller, was indicted for refusing to register for the military draft which had been reinstated in the United States. About forty persons, including Sister Anna, gathered on the day of his trial before the US District Court in Roanoke, Virginia, to lend their support before his arraignment. Speaking to the media and others gathered there, Anna contrasted Eller's indictment to the innocent verdict which had been recently rendered in the trial of John Hinckley who was being tried for the attempted assassination of the President of the United States. With eyes flashing and upraised arm Anna asserted:

> If you want to be free in this country, shoot the President, and the government will do everything possible to be fair to you. We are against a wall with our law that spends a fortune to keep one man out of jail, and today may put another in jail.

Three weeks later, at his request, she stood by young Eller's side in Wichita, Kansas, as he appeared before the members participating in the Annual Conference of the Church of the Brethren. Every one of the 3,500 persons present that afternoon realized that he faced a possible prison sentence of five years plus $10,000 fine for the stand he had taken. After a standing ovation for the two of them, Enten spoke eloquently but quietly of his deeply held convictions and then led Sister Anna from the stage with his arm affectionately about her shoulders. It was a moving, never-to-be-forgotten moment for those present and there were few dry eyes when they made their somber exit.

True, it is a crazy, mixed-up world in which Sister Anna

finds herself in her golden years but she continues to speak out courageously and emphatically for the values of the One to Whom she has given a lifetime of service. And, much to her great joy, there are evidences of substantial support from many world-recognized figures for the values which she has held so dear. There is no contemporary world figure, however, who has so challenged, amused and amazed Sister Anna as has the English writer, Malcolm Muggeridge. Although the two of them did not meet until she was past eighty and he was in his late seventies, there was an instantaneous mutual bond between them: It was their love for and belief in the Person of Jesus Christ.

Born in 1903 and brought up in a Fabian Socialist family, Muggeridge was one of England's most controversial and brilliant journalists. Described as a man with a razor-sharp wit, passionate moral convictions and unsentimental common sense one of his friends declared that he had made a brilliant career of shocking the English-speaking world. An accomplished author, playwright and newspaper man, Muggeridge is believed by many to be the finest writer of English prose in his generation. At the least he was the most prolific! "For more than half a century," he once asserted, "I've been a 'vendor of words' — millions and millions of them — I have let loose a positive Niagara of words, frothing and churning on their tumultous course."

His career included work on a number of English newspapers throughout the world as well as university teaching posts in both India and Egypt. During World War II, he won many decorations, including the Legion of Honor, for his service as a Major in the Intelligence Corp. Following the war, he lived in Washington for a period of time as a correspondent for the *Daily Telegram,* and this was followed by a five-year stint as the editor of *Punch,* the slick, sophisticated British humor magazine. A fellow journalist at that time described his editorial style as "sharp, urbane, agile mockery. Nothing was sacred."

Agnostic and cynic that he was, Muggeridge had little interest in religion until he was past sixty years of age except to poke fun on occasion at what he sometimes referred to as "trendy clergymen" and "deluded intellectuals."

But, according to his own admission in later life, there was always a feeling of lostness, of not being totally at home in this world—a belief that there was something more than the shallow, superficial life which had been symptomatic of his varied and distinguished career. One might say that for him there was no dramatic Damascus-road type of conversion but rather a gradual movement from atheism to that of being an ardent, nondenominational Christian.

In 1954, Muggeridge did a series of TV shows for the British Broadcasting Company (BBC) in which he interviewed many famous personalities from all walks of life. The very first guest was Billy Graham, the world-reknowned evangelist. Neither of them would have dreamed at that time that 20 years later Graham would introduce Muggeridge as "my dear friend and fellow Christian" to more than 3,000 persons at the International Congress on World Evangelism in Switzerland. By 1974, Muggeridge was considered by some of his former friends as a "snowy-thatched Jesus freak," while others declared him to be the "prophet to a shallow culture." The Rev. John R. W. Stott gave the most clear-cut contemporary view of him when he said: "The reality of Jesus Christ shines brightly in Malcolm Muggeridge." His rebirth was a long process. It was a 20-year, step-by-step saga of one who reached Reality via the light shed on the pathway by the lives of hundreds who had gone before.

Describing himself as a "theological ignoramus," Muggeridge began his pilgrimage to discover more about the life of Christ after going to Palestine to film a documentary on that land for the BBC. While there he was appalled at the tawdry commercialism surrounding many of the shrines sacred to the beginning of Christianity, and he said so. But he could not lightly dismiss the looks on the faces of the pilgrims, the impact made on him by the Sea of Galilee, the surrounding wilderness, the hills of Bethlehem and the very air of Palestine. All of these stirred his imagination about the Person of One who had been born two thousand years before and who still held such sway over the hearts and minds of so many of the world's people.

Prompted by insatiable curiosity stemming from his

own specific genius with words, he became obsessed with a study of *the* Word, God's. The more he studied the more fascinated he became. The sharp, incisive writings of St. Paul especially intrigued him and he decided to do a five-part documentary TV series on the life of St. Paul. Here was a man after his own mold. He must know him better.

Together with a friend of his college years, Dr. Alec Vidler (now Dean of King's College, Cambridge University), Muggeridge embarked on an arduous two months of travel, following Paul's journeys between Jerusalem and Rome. Theirs was an attempt to try to understand what Paul stood for, what he meant to them, and what his teachings could mean for contemporary civilization. Through the eyes of these two old friends, so totally different in their personalities as well as in their past fifty years of living, there emerged a St. Paul whose message to the 20th century is as valid as when he wrote his letters to the young churches more than two thousand years ago. The TV documentary and a subsequent book, *Paul, Envoy Extraordinary,* produced a contemporary picture of the life of St. Paul that will not be equaled in our generation. By now, Muggeridge was captured. There was no doubt where Reality was to be found.

The next step on his own personal pilgrimage involved the study of six more individuals who had been instrumental in the preservation of the torch of Jesus' teachings that they might be passed on to future generations. He saw these six—St. Augustine, Blaise Pascal, William Blake, Soren Kierkegaard, Leo Tolstoy and Dietrich Bonhoeffer—as a continuing testament to the reality of God that stretched back through both the Old and New Testaments. The studying of these six evolved into another television series entitled *The Third Testament,* later to be reproduced in a book of the same title.

Anna's meeting of Malcolm Muggeridge was one of those happy coincidences of fate that often come about in undreamt-of ways. The Muggeridges live in a 400-year-old English cottage only a short distance from the Bruderhof center in Sussex, England, where Anna's and Baxter's son, Merrill, made his home at that time. On a visit to see Merrill's family in December, 1979, Anna happened to be seated by Kitty Muggeridge, Malcolm's wife, at a tea which Kathy, Merrill's wife, was giving for some of her neighbors. Children, grandchildren and their mutual interests in many things provided some lively conversation between the two. Upon telling Mrs. Muggeridge goodbye that afternoon, Anna remarked in her typically frank fashion: "You tell your husband I'd like to meet him some day—not because he is so famous and well-known but because he loves my Lord Jesus!" Whereupon Mrs. Muggeridge replied with warm delight and hearty laughter: "Malcolm will *love* that!" Before she left England Anna was invited to the Muggeridges for tea and was to see the study where Muggeridge's "Niagara of words" poured forth. Their joy in meeting each other was mutual.

In January of 1981, Anna and her sister Lois returned to England for another visit with her son and they were once again invited to tea at the Muggeridge home. There was much of Anna's "holy hilarity" present on that occasion along with the serious talk. When Muggeridge's wife of 54 years was asked once by a reporter what she most appreciated about her husband, she replied without hesitation: "Malcolm's goodness and his sense of humor. He still makes me laugh!" The keen sense of humor shared by both Anna and Muggeridge, their mutual zest for life, for words, for people and for ideas, plus the delightful English confections prepared by Mrs. Muggeridge made that a never-to-be-forgotten experience.

In spite of this remarkable computerized, mechanical age in which we live, the best way to package an important message is still through the lives and words of persons. Modern tools and technology are of real value in expanding and making known the message, but the love, the compassion and the mercy of God are still best revealed through the lives of those who are His own. Sister Anna saw the kingdom of Heaven coming, not through the planning and machinations of organized religion but through the yeasty method of revealing God's way in day-by-day personal contacts with both friends *and* enemies. She saw the hard-won fruits of the spirit—patience, forgiveness, agape love—as products of a process of intentional growth, not as an instantaneous change bestowed in a miraculous spiritual happening which required no further effort on the part of the recipient.

The thousands of letters which she had received from individuals for more than half a century were clear indication to her that the so-called "institutional church" as many persons knew it was not always ministering to their most deeply felt spiritual needs. *Somehow the church must become the church as the body of Christ in the world; the inner man and the outer man must become as one because the mind of Christ had come into a person's very being.* Developing this "mind of Christ" within her own person became her magnificent obsession, and sharing this belief with a sin-sick world was her reason for being. "I believe with all my heart that this is the greatest day the Christian church has ever seen," she announced triumphantly in her 88th year, "for the Christian message and life is the most relevant answer to this crazy world's needs."

This passionately held belief was not held by Sister Anna alone. There were others—many of them—sharing the same sentiment but few could articulate it quite so well as her friend Malcolm Muggeridge. With his usual flair for words, and perhaps in an attempt to make up for some lost time in his own life, there came from his small study in Sussex a veritable landslide of books, articles, interviews and statements to underlie and bring to the world his own basis beliefs. In 1980, there appeared a small book based on two lectures delivered by Muggeridge at the University of Waterloo in October of 1978. The lectures, *The End of Christendom* and *But Not of Christ,* were followed by a discussion in which he explained that Christendom is something quite different from Christianity. Christ said his Kingdom is not of this world; Christendom, on the other hand, *is* of this world and, like every other human creation, subject to decay, change and possible eventual desolation. All Christians may not share his pessimistic view of Christendom—but few would disagree with the following keen analysis of the world's ills and Jesus Christ as the ultimate answer to those ills.

God has mercifully made the fantasies—the pursuit of power, of sensual satisfaction, of money, of learning, of celebrity, of happiness—so preposterously unrewarding that we are forced to turn to him for help and for mercy. We seek wealth and we find we've accumulated worthless pieces of paper. We seek security and find we've acquired the means to blow ourselves and our little earth to smithereens. We seek carnal indulgence only to find ourselves involved in the prevailing erotomania. Looking for freedom, we infallibly fall in the servitude of self-gratification or, collectively of a Gulag Archipelago . . . .

We look back on history and what do we see? Empires rising and falling, revolutions and counter revolutions, wealth accumulating and wealth disbursed, one nation dominant and then another . . . . By identifying ourselves with Christ, by absorbing his teaching, by living out the drama of his life with him, including the passion, that powerhouse of love and creativity—by living with, by and in him, we can be reborn to become new men and new women in a new world . . . . This is a fulfillment that transcends all human fulfilling and yet is accessible to all humans, based on the absolutes of love rather than the relativities of justice, on the universality of brotherhood rather than the particularity of equality, on the perfect service which is freedom rather than the perfect servitude which purports to be freedom . . . . We become forgetful that Jesus is the prophet of the losers' not the victors' camp, the one who proclaims that the first will be last, that the weak are the strong and the fools are the wise . . . . Let us then as Christians rejoice that we see around us on every hand the decay of institutions and instruments of power, see intimations of empires falling to pieces, money in total disarray, dictators and parliamentarians alike nonplussed by the confusions and conflicts which encompass them. For it is precisely when every earthly hope has been explored and found wanting, when every possibility of help from earthly sources has been sought and is not forthcoming, when every recourse this world offers, moral as well as material, has been explored to no effect, when in the shivering cold the last faggot has been thrown on the fire and in the gathering darkness every glimmer of light has finally flickered out, it's then that Christ's hand reaches out sure and firm. Then Christ's words bring their inexpressible comfort, then his light shines brightest, abolishing the darkness forever. So, finding in everything only deception and nothingness, the soul is constrained to have recourse to God himself and to rest content with him.

There may be some who would disagree with the eminent Mr. Muggeridge on individual issues or statements but few would disagree with the fact that he has been one of the most astute observers of the world scene in this century and as such his observations merit our attention. His own witness and that of others named in this chapter were an important part of Sister Anna's own faith journey. Why? Because they, too, shared her vision of creation as a continuing and ongoing process from century to century. And also because they deeply believed in the way of the cross and of self-giving love as being the final answer to the sins that confront each new age. Sister Anna's faith journey was not a lonely one. Neither are we alone. There are, and will continue to be, a host of those who share that "wild hope," that "faith tremendous."

Anna is an inveterate note writer, not only to herself but to others. Old envelopes, scraps of paper, backs of church bulletins, program copies, napkins—anything and everything is used for recording. Her sense of humor asserted itself once in what she declared to be the *longest* note she ever wrote. It was a letter sent to Baxter from Egypt and it was written in her large, scrawling penmanship on thirty nine inches of Egyptian toilet tissue! More recently, when Anna was prevented by illness from participating in the 1982 Church of the Brethren National Youth Conference, she wrote a note to the 3,000 young people on a paper towel, the only thing handy to her hospital bed!

Like a dampened sponge she soaks up every little incident and illustration she observes or hears and stores it away in that computer-like brain of hers to be retrieved at any time to drive home a point that needs special emphasis. Her faculty for doing this is incredible to her friends, but no doubt some of it is due to the constant notes she makes. Reading through her speeches, articles, books and numerous notes there emerges a thought that appears over and over again. It is almost like the theme melody in a symphony that repeats itself again and again in unexpected places and from unexpected instruments. The idea so weaves itself into the fabric of her thinking that it might be aptly named her own theme song: "But it is through the love of God that I am what I am, AND THE LOVE THAT HE SHOWED ME HAS NOT BEEN WASTED (1 Cor. 15:10, Phillips)." Sister Anna's rich full life stands as an eternal testimony to the fact that her theme has been played out in majestic cadence.

Epilogue

"What is it really like to get to know Anna Mow deeply?" "How did you decide what to include and what not to include in writing about her?" Both questions were asked of me during the three years I did the necessary research and writing of this book. This epilogue is an attempt to answer those questions and to write of the impact of the project on my own personal life during this period.

The process of putting words on paper about any human being, living or dead, is a challenging one and not to be taken lightly. I did not take this assignment lightly. Why? Because at the very outset Anna made it clear to me that whatever was written should magnify and honor her Lord and not her. Some people who know her best feel that Anna and her Lord are inseparable; to know and love one is to know and love the other. Be that as it may, the two of us mutually agreed upon the concept of making what she *stood* for the most important element of her story, not merely a recital of the details of her life. With this in mind, I began the process of getting to know her in depth. It was an exciting, rewarding, challenging and sometimes exasperating and frustrating experience.

It was exciting because I learned so much. I learned that Anna's was an *intentional* life, one dedicated to a lifelong search for truth, tolerance, and integrity. I learned from her that people must first deal with what is wrong in themselves before they are ready to work effectively for the fulfillment God's purposes through their efforts. For her, this meant self-denial, servanthood, and in some instances "climbing up on the cross." It meant agape love. "The greatest blessing of God comes when we allow ourselves not to be argued or coaxed, but to be *loved* into the Kingdom," she reminded me, not once but many times.

Anna was her own sternest judge and she was ever ready to leave the discipline and the judgment of others to the Holy Spirit as God's earthly representative. I learned from her that one should seek a balance between a realistic faith and chasing the rainbows of unreality which tend to deny the pain and perils of our ordinary human existence. She did not see true religion as an escape from reality with all of the rewards coming like "pie in the sky" at some future date. She saw true religion as going foward in faith and courage in the most trying of circumstances under the guidance of an ever-present and ever-loving Spirit.

I learned that Anna *was* what she taught. There was an unquestioning commitment to the search for carrying out the will of God for her life. With her there was only one question: "What is my Father's will?" No doubt that accounted for the singleness of mind and purpose that enabled her to accomplish so much.

I learned that her desire to live her life totally within the context of God's will was not a mere happenstance. It was a deliberate choice, a decision made in early adulthood as a result of her nurture when a child. She had been wrapped snugly within the blankets of a patriarchal society that nourished a family atmosphere of learning and intellectual pursuits, but with the added priceless dimension of a dedication to the Divine within. Generous and warm-hearted by nature, her magnificent obsession was to give back to her Creator the very best and most she had to offer.

Anna was a strong-willed, individualistic human being and such persons do not usually give up their rights to themselves easily. They have as much struggle as anyone, perhaps even more than many, in making themselves completely subservient to the "will" of another, even of their Creator. But in the doing of His will, in living life in complete obedience to His direction, they find the freedom which enables them to be a blessing to Him as well as others.

Writing about Anna was a rewarding experience for me because one seldom has the opportunity for an in depth discovery of the knowledge and experience of one who has lived so long and so richly. I listened to the stories she shared about people from many different cultures, stories lifting up their "oneness" as human beings, their needs, their struggles. There was never a breach of confidence, as names were never used nor privacy invaded. Some of the stories had happy endings, some did not, but all added up to the rich mosaic that had been her life. I felt privileged to be made aware of both the joy and pain that had been hers in years of profound ministry to the deepest needs of persons.

It was a challenge to get to know her in depth because I discovered that her entire life was a clarion call to follow the Master whom she served, even to the cross if that proved necessary. Anna did not believe in "cheap grace" or easy assignments. She challenged one to accept whatever disciplines, whatever sacrifices that were necessary in order that the living Christ might become the Presence within. Her conviction that this was the only answer to the needs of a hurting world was a profound one. She spoke to me often of the need for the church to become the "body of Christ" in the world. And she had a deep concern for the fact that the mechanics of keeping the institutional church in gear sometimes prevented it from serving as the vehicle whereby we could discover the mind of Christ in dealing with the day-by-day problems and deepest spiritual and emotional needs of its members.

Listening to Anna and writing about her was exasperating at times because I felt keenly my own incompetency to fully absorb what she had to share and then transfer the same ideas into a coherent and readable form. Tape recordings helped, but they also hindered in the free flow of ideas and thoughts between us as we struggled with the necessary mechanics of operation. There also was exasperation because the two of us frequently had difficulty staying on an assigned topic or question. One thought would lead to another and suddenly we would find ourselves far, far afield from what we originally set out to discuss! But I found her mind so keen, her insights so sharp and incisive and her thinking process so disciplined that we were soon back on course, more often at her instigation than my own.

Frustration arose for me over what to include, what to delete. The stories she shared about her life the ideas, the gems of thought about living which came out in frequent telephone conversations and short visits—all of them taught me something and I felt that somehow they must be included in the manuscript. I soon discovered, however, that making a selection from the smorgasbord of riches she spread before me was imperative if the book was to be kept to a readable length. There were also some things we shared that she felt should not be made public because of the pain it could bring to the lives of living persons. This I respected.

The period during which this book was being written was a trying time for both of us. Anna was hospitalized several times with a serious heart condition and with two operations on her eyes for cataracts. Frequently when I stopped by to see her she was in real pain but throughout the entire time there was never a word of self-pity nor was the age-old question of those who suffer asked: "Why me?" She was frustrated, of course, and sometimes discouraged that she could not be about her usual busy routine of travel and speaking engagements. Her greatest disappointment was not being able to attend the 1982 National Youth Conference of the Church of the Brethren to which she had looked forward with great anticipation for several years. She sent them a message written on four paper towels from her hospital bed. The youth reciprocated with a giant get-well card on which they inscribed their own loving thoughts and wishes for her recovery.

Her most severe trial was the inability to read. She, who often read several books each week as well as numerous magazines and the daily paper, was now cut off from the things which meant most in her life, yet there was not a murmuring word. Her radio and records provided hours of beautiful music, and with these and the telephone calls from friends throughout the country she managed for the most part to keep up her radiant spirit. There was scarcely a time that I stopped by that she did not provide me with some stimulating thought, some new and bright courage for living.

Within weeks of completing the manuscript I was faced with the most catastrophic event in my own life that had happened to date. Although I did not share my own pain with her because of her weakened condition, she gave me the message I most needed to hear as I left her that day: "Don't forget, Dotty, no matter what may ever happen to you, *God is there*, and He is faithful." And I knew from that moment that whatever decisions were reached, they would be made to a large degree because of what I had learned from her during the past three years.

It has been said that the primary reason for human existence is that we might "glorify God and enjoy Him forever." If that is true, then Sister Anna's life was truly a fulfillment of God's hope for each individual member of the human family. In the words of Oswald Chambers, her life was "an absolute paean of perfectly irrepressible, triumphant belief." Such persons are as rare as rainbows in the kaleidoscopic shuffle of humanity to which most of us will be exposed down through the years of our lives. The message of her life is an important one. It is timeless. It is for now, it is for eternity. In a Christmas letter she wrote in recent years, these lines were included, lines which are an invitation to us to share in the joyous adventure that was hers in living:

> Let us not leave God in his loneliness—
> *Let us not waste His love.*
> Let us become His instruments, imperfect,
> Dull as we may be. In His hands,
> Measured by His standards
> We go forth.

Finis

D.G.M.
Nov. 28, 1982